Tibetan Yogas of Body, Speech, and Mind

Tibetan Yogas of Body, Speech, and Mind

Tenzin Wangyal Rinpoche
Edited by Polly Turner

SNOW LION PUBLICATIONS
ITHACA, NEW YORK

Snow Lion Publications
P.O. Box 6483
Ithaca, New York 14851 USA
(607) 273-8519 www.snowlionpub.com

Printed in USA on acid-free recycled paper.

ISBN-10: 1-55939-380-7
ISBN-13: 978-1-55939-380-5

Library of Congress Cataloging-in-Publication Data

Wangyal, Tenzin.
  Tibetan yogas of body, speech, and mind / Tenzin Wangyal
Rinpoche ; edited by Polly Turner.
      p. cm.
  Includes index.
  ISBN-13: 978-1-55939-380-5 (alk. paper)
  ISBN-10: 1-55939-380-7 (alk. paper)
  1. Yoga—Bon (Tibetan religion) I. Turner, Polly, 1953- II. Title.
BQ7982.2.W35 2011
299.5'4—dc22

                                                        2011010775

Designed and typeset by Gopa & Ted2, Inc.

This book is dedicated to my teacher
Yongdzin Tenzin Namdak Rinpoche

Contents

Illustrations

PLATES

TABLES

Preface

WHEN I was a young monk in Dolanji, India, nearly every morning for three years I would join a small group of older students in the house of my root teacher Lopön Sangyé Tenzin Rinpoche and listen to his explanations from the *Oral Transmission of Zhang Zhung* (*Zhang Zhung Nyen Gyü*).

Lopön Sangyé Tenzin lived a very simple, solitary life in his isolated residence, seldom even leaving his bedroom. Yet, he was considered by many to be the greatest Bön scholar of his generation. Lopön delivered the dzogchen teachings of the *Oral Transmission* in a very clear, direct, and strict manner, rarely allowing even one question. It was hard work, but it was wonderful, too.

For eleven years at the Bön Dialectics School of Menri Monastery, I engaged in rigorous training in epistemology, cosmology, sutra, tantra, and dzogchen under the guidance of Lopön and other masters from the Bön and Buddhist schools of Tibet. Back then I always assumed that when it came time for me to teach I would duplicate the traditional presentation, moving chapter by chapter and point by point through the ancient texts, just as Lopön and countless other masters over the centuries had done before me. But once I attained my geshé degree and began to teach in Europe and then in the United States, I was troubled to find a general lack of committed engagement among my Western students.

Some students would base their decision to come to a retreat not on the opportunity to be with me and receive the precious dharma but rather on the specific topic I would be teaching about. If they had already received those teachings or if the teaching was on sutra or tantra and they wanted dzogchen, they might decide not to come. Others would come and tell me how connected they felt to the teachings and to me, but after a few months or years, I would never see them again. One student whom I hadn't seen in several years returned to greet me and announced that he had found skydiving. Somehow he had progressed from the profound, esoteric dzogchen meditation practice of sky gazing to the sport of skydiving!

The more I have learned from my twenty years of living and teaching in the West, the more I have come to see how these attitudes are grounded in cultural upbringing and education as well as in the everyday constraints of Western life. It is not always easy for people here to practice meditation in a dedicated way. Many conditions have to be met: There must be the financial and other means to set aside time away from work and family obligations. There must be a quiet, peaceful, inspiring environment.

What is more, I have learned that for many Westerners a strictly traditional approach to the study of the dharma can itself be an obstacle to understanding and continuous engagement in the practices. Although the knowledge contained in the ancient texts is timeless and as valuable now as it has ever been, the Bön Buddhist teachings were originally tailored to students from a different culture and different centuries. For this reason, over the years I have increasingly focused on translating the dharma in such a way that it resonates clearly with modern Western values, sensibilities, and day-to-day life.

Preserving Ancient Knowledge

Importantly, I am also dedicated to ensuring that these teachings are communicated with no alterations to their original meaning. Bön is the indigenous culture and indigenous spiritual tradition of Tibet. It predates Tibetan Buddhism, which was introduced to Tibet from India in the seventh century. It also predates Buddhism itself, tracing its spiritual heritage to Tönpa Shenrab Miwoché, a buddha born thousands of years earlier than Shakyamuni Buddha. The Bön teachings have been transmitted from teacher to teacher from ancient times through to Nyamé Shérab Gyeltsen, the fourteenth-century founder and first abbot of Menri Monastery in Central Tibet, and then to the masters of this modern time.

Helping to preserve these precious teachings for the benefit of future generations requires that the initiations, transmissions, and specifications of the instructions remain pure and unchanged and that the shared knowledge and experience of these teachings remain genuine. Therefore, I have been extremely careful not to create something new, or to mix and match different teachings, or to impart a wrong view by leaving out a key understanding. Instead I have simplified traditional practices to permit students to find themselves where they are, providing a clear map so that they can connect in ever-deeper ways until they can recognize the best of themselves, their essential nature. Before I present significant changes, I always check with my teachers.

MANY PATHS TO ENLIGHTENMENT

The teachings and practices of Bön permit direct experiential insight into the human mind. Ultimately, Bön offers a complete path to enlightenment. As Bön Buddhist practitioners, we practice meditation not only to relieve mundane suffering and conflicts but also as a spiritual path for this lifetime and for beyond this life as well. Practicing meditation is a means of liberating not only ourselves but all beings from all the causes of suffering. This is why we recite a prayer of compassion at the start of every meditation session and dedicate the merits of our practice to all beings at the close of each session.

Everybody is looking for happiness and the causes of happiness, and everybody wants relief from suffering and the causes of suffering. Yet we usually look for happiness and relief of suffering in all the wrong places and in all the wrong ways. The root of suffering is the self-grasping mind from which attachment, aversion, and other afflictive emotions arise. Every negative action of our body, speech, or mind that is based in this self-grasping mind creates a seed of karma, a habitual tendency that traps us from one lifetime to the next in a cycle of suffering known as samsara. To help reveal an end to this cycle, this book draws on a vast system of knowledge to show the many ways that body, speech, and mind can instead be utilized as doorways to happiness, contentment, better health, and ultimately liberation.

Bön has practices that give access to a deep connection with love, compassion, and other higher qualities. It also has practices that promote a sacred, healing relationship with the natural world. Bön's shamanic rituals and customs pervade not only Bön Buddhism but also the four major schools of Tibetan Buddhism. As with many other indigenous cultures, the people of Tibet tend to have a deep sense of connection to the spirits of mountains, rivers, and other facets of nature. The shamanic teachings are rich and beautiful and profoundly empowering. Yet from the point of view of the Bön Buddhist teachings, the shamanic perspective is limited because it is based so strongly on physical form. In Bön we refer to our shamanic traditions as the causal vehicles since despite their limitations, they can serve as a steppingstone to the higher Bön teachings of sutra, tantra, and dzogchen and thus can be a cause of higher realization.

The sutra, tantra, and dzogchen of Bön share a great deal in common with the teachings of the same name found within the four major schools of Tibetan Buddhism.

Sutra, known as the "path of renunciation," offers many rules of conduct that support our overcoming the negative habits and tendencies that hinder attainment of enlightenment.

Tantra, the "path of transformation," relies primarily on two key stages of practice—the generation and perfection stages—to transform grosser experiences of the body, energy, and mind into subtler experiences. Like sutra, its teachings and practices have their origins in the teachings of the buddhas. Tantra is often misconstrued by Westerners. While it is true that some tantric practices do indeed work with the experience of sexuality, their goal is not just sexual pleasure, it is to transform these grosser levels of attachment and desire into the more subtle, sacred experiences of open bliss and finally into the subtlest experience of open awareness.

Dzogchen, also known as the "great perfection" or "great completion" teaching, is considered the path of self-liberation. Unlike sutra or tantra, dzogchen does not require anything to be renounced or transformed. Rather, every experience of body, speech, and mind need only be recognized for what it truly is: complete and perfect in itself. Dzogchen is considered the highest teaching and practice in both Bön and the Nyingma school of Tibetan Buddhism.

Some of the teachings in this book, particularly those related to dzogchen and tantra, were until recently held in strict secrecy both as a sign of respect and as a protection against their being diluted through the misunderstanding of unprepared practitioners. They were never taught publicly or given lightly but were reserved for individuals who had prepared to receive them. In times past, suitable vessels were willing to travel far on foot and endure other great hardships to access these teachings. But this is seldom the case now; and to preserve the teachings we are challenged to bring them to a new, global audience. My teacher Lopön Sangyé Tenzin Rinpoche advised me that it is time to teach openly. I believe there are some people who simply will not understand, no matter how clearly you teach, and that the goddess is keeping the teachings secret from them. We must trust that the teachings will inevitably reach the right vessels and that what is meant to be kept secret will remain so.

It is my deepest wish that by conveying openly and simply what is effective, many more people will benefit; that Bön's rich cultural heritage will be preserved for centuries to come; and that its lineage of teachers, wisdom teachings, and transmissions will continue unbroken as it has since ancient times.

Maintaining an Unbroken Lineage

Preserving this tradition remains a monumental task as Bön is under a continual threat of extinction. During the Chinese Cultural Revolution, countless Bön monasteries, religious texts, ritual items, and artwork were destroyed. My root teacher Lopön Sangyé Tenzin, who passed away in 1978 at age 67, was one of only three elder lineage masters to escape Tibet alive amid the violence and destruction. The other two are His Holiness Lungtok Tenpai Nyima, the current spiritual head of the Bön tradition and abbot of Menri Monastery in India, and Yongdzin Tenzin Namdak Rinpoche, the foremost living teacher of the Bön tradition, who is my other root teacher and who raised me like his own son from the time of my early adolescence. These three served as my main teachers, along with Lharampa Geshé Yungdrung Namgyel, my primary master in philosophy as I studied for my geshé degree.

It is only through the struggles of these three great masters in exile that so many of the Bön teachings have remained intact and are available now to the world. In exile new monasteries were established, and seeds of knowledge were planted in a handful of younger students who in time would be called on to help preserve the Bön tradition for future generations.

As one of those students, I have tried to do what I can toward this end. In 1992 I founded Ligmincha Institute in Charlottesville, Virginia (www.ligmincha.org), and six years later I established the Serenity Ridge retreat center thirty minutes south of Charlottesville in Nelson County. Ligmincha's goal is to introduce the ancient traditions in an authentic manner to the Western world, in such a way that they remain beneficial when integrated into modern Western culture. Ligmincha also aims to preserve and further develop the indigenous culture of Tibet, both among Tibetans living in exile and among interested Westerners. I have also established many affiliated Ligmincha and Chamma Ling centers worldwide and am in the process of founding Lishu Institute, a residential center in India where Western students can engage in long-term study and practice and where the Bön Buddhist teachings may be preserved as literature, transmission, and knowledge.

I have additionally seen a need to open the Bön teachings to a wider audience, including people who do not necessarily see themselves as Bön practitioners and even those who are only looking for practical methods to improve their lives or to support their work in the healing professions. Toward this end, with the blessings of Yongdzin Tenzin Namdak Rinpoche and His Holiness Lungtok Tenpai Nyima Rinpoche, I have helped to initiate a training program called The Three Doors. In time I hope this effort will permit many more people to benefit from the ancient wisdom teachings.

PRESERVATION THROUGH PRACTICE

Gaining knowledge is an important part of the spiritual path, and there are endless possibilities for expanding one's intellectual learning. Yet the conceptual mind has a way of creating a lot of confusion, doubt, and distress, and the entire intellectual path tends to become a question in search of a single answer. Ultimately, the answer itself is beyond the reach of the intellect.

I feel that I have had some success in presenting the quintessential points of the teachings and providing a means to direct experience through effective practice. For me, a successful retreat is when people from a variety of different intellectual backgrounds and levels of meditative experience feel a collective benefit in meditation practice. Their training and intellectual understanding may differ, but in the experiential aspect all divisions are dissolved: everyone participating arrives at a single place.

Is it possible to have genuine experience without going through many years of intellectual training? The answer is yes. The process begins with receiving the wisdom teachings known as the dharma. But hearing or reading about the teachings is not enough. Neither is reflecting on what you have heard or having good intentions to practice meditation. Many people feel that because they go to retreats and accumulate knowledge they are good practitioners, but the teaching cannot ripen in you until you actually practice it and your practice begins to deepen. Your ability to experience the great bliss that comes from recognition of your true nature depends on nothing but practice.

By helping you discover a deep source of knowledge and wisdom, meditation practice can bring you to the sense of connection, completion, and fulfillment that you yearn for. Ultimately, it can help you arrive at the more profound sense of peace and happiness that comes only from connecting with your deeper essence.

Ideally, you should be open to the infinite possibility of intellectual learning but not get lost in it. Through study combined with practice, you can gain direct experience of the truth in the simplest of places: within your own body, speech, and mind.

Acknowledgments

I WISH TO offer my heartfelt thanks to the many people who contributed their time and effort to the creation of this book, which has been so many years in the making. In particular I thank managing editor Sidney Piburn and copy editor Michael Wakoff of Snow Lion Publications for their care and expertise in overseeing the book's completion. Other individuals who generously reviewed the draft and offered valuable improvements include Alejandro Chaoul-Reich, Scott Clearwater, Patricia Gift, Steven Goodman, Andrew Lukianowicz, Steve Roth, Laura Shekerjian, and Gabriel Rocco.

I thank those who generously contributed images for the book, including Geshé Nyima Gyeltsen, for his illustration of the White Liquid Practice to Heal Disease; Lhari-la Kelzang Nyima, for his illustration of the channels and chakras; Timothy Arbon, for his illustration of the three root channels; Rogelio Jaramillo Flores, for his photographs of the five-point meditation posture, prostration, and White Liquid Practice to Heal Disease; Tom Maroshegyi, for his photographs of Tibetan yoga postures; and Janine Guldener, for her photographs of the tsa lung movements. Alejandro Chaoul-Reich, who regularly teaches Tibetan yoga at my request to students around the world, kindly demonstrated the trulkhor movements in chapter 4.

I extend my appreciation to His Eminence Menri Lopön Trinley Nyima Rinpoche and Geshé Samten Tsukphu for being available to clear the essential doubts of various points; and to Kurt Keutzer and William Gorvine for confirming the accuracy of information.

I am especially grateful to my longtime student Polly Turner who, with a lot of openness, patience, and energy, has worked with me so closely on this project. From the time that the idea for the book germinated until its physical manifestation, she has been drafting and editing its words very closely with me, and without her the book would not have been possible. I am thankful as well for Polly's continual availability to assist with Ligmincha Institute's communication needs and with so many of the other creative projects that have been flowing around me.

Finally, I wish to thank my wife, Khandro Tsering Wangmo, for her love and care, her patience during my frequent absences, her open generosity in hosting all the visitors to our home and our lives, and her devotion in caring for our son Senghe. It is only through her support that I am able to accomplish all that I do.

Tenzin Wangyal

Kathmandu, Nepal, February 5, 2011

Introduction

All pure virtue done through the three doors,
I dedicate to the welfare of all sentient beings
    of the three realms.
After having purified all afflictions and obscurations
    of the three poisons,
May we swiftly achieve the complete buddhahood
    of the three bodies.[1]

IN THE TIBETAN Bön Buddhist tradition, these lines are a prayer we recite at the close of every ritual and meditation session. As we say them, we are dedicating all our virtuous actions done through the three doors of body, speech, and mind to the enlightenment of ourselves and all beings.

Body, speech, and mind are considered the three doors to enlightenment not just in Bön but in all the major spiritual traditions of Tibet for they are the only tools we have for progressing on the spiritual path.

When we know how to work skillfully with them, our own body, speech, and mind offer a constant opportunity to reflect and connect with the joyful, formless truth that is our authentic nature. The physical, energetic, and mental realms of our experience are always with us. Not only are they within us, we are part of them. They *are* who we are:

1. The three doors refer to body, speech, and mind; the three realms, to the desire, form, and formless realms; the three poisons, to aversion, desire, and ignorance; the three bodies (or dimensions), to the *dharmakaya* (*bönku*), the *sambhogakaya* (*dzogku, longku*), and the *nirmanakaya* (*trülku*).

there is nothing closer to us than the three doors. No matter where we are or what we are doing, we can enter through the body into the higher experiences of *eternal body*, through speech into *ceaseless speech*, and through mind into *undeluded mind*.

SMALL SELF, BIG SELF

I often say that these three doors can be used not only as an entrance but also as an exit. It is easy to observe how the conditions of body, speech, and mind can cloud the awareness. All it may take is a mild head cold, a wrong word said in haste, or a moment of anger to obscure our clarity of thought and divert us farther away from our heart, from our soul, from our deepest wishes for happiness and satisfaction.

In the absolute sense, what we hope to find through the three doors of body, speech, and mind is self-realization: realization of who we truly are. Buddhism says there is no inherent self, no inherent reality; but just as every phenomenon exists, but not inherently, the self also exists, but not inherently. In dzogchen, we say "self-introduction"—introduction to your self. Who we really are is the unconditional experience of being, in the absence of the grasping mind. Who we are not is what we usually identify with, for example, "I am a mother," "I am a lawyer." We identify with our roles, our thoughts, our emotions, or other conditions we are trapped in. When we go beyond that mistaken view of self, we can discover who we truly are: the inseparable state of openness and awareness.

But before we can begin to understand this larger self, we need to explore who we are in the smaller sense. Who is the one here, now, the one who is manifesting in this identity through body, speech, and mind?

Sometimes I may have a very positive sense of identity, other times I may view myself as someone quite terrible. Somebody is here, but who is it? Am I the one who appears terrible, or am I the one who perceives the terrible identity? When I speak, am I the words I say, or am I the one who intends to speak? If I feel sick, am I the body that is sick, or am I the one who is aware of the sick body? Who am I?

We can ask ourselves questions like these in order to understand the sense of self we may have at any given moment. Most of the time our view of ourselves causes us pain. We feel the pain of needing and desiring what we don't have, the pain of fear or anxiety over losing what we do have, the pain of being separated from our loved ones, the pain of encountering our enemies.

The main causes of this pain and suffering are the conceptual mind, karmic conditions, and negative emotions. The teachings speak of an enlightened sense of body, speech, and mind, but for now, in the negative sense we can be said to have a *conceptual-karmic-emotional pain body, conceptual-karmic-emotional pain speech*, and a *conceptual-karmic-emotional pain mind*. I refer to these three more simply as "pain body," "pain speech," and "pain mind."

The Tibetan spiritual traditions use the term *pain body*, or *body of suffering (dungel gyi phungpo)* in contrast with the term *changeless bliss body (gyurwa mépa déchen gyi ku)*. Eckhart Tolle, the renowned author and spiritual teacher, has additionally offered a simple and direct explanation of the pain body that I find inspiring. As the pain body is such an essential concept, I have expanded it to incorporate the notion of pain speech and pain mind.

Whether physically, energetically, or psychologically, we experience ourselves mainly through our pain. It is hard to recognize *rigpa*, the enlightened nature that is our self, the nature that we share with the deities. The small self is more familiar to us. The small self is the one through which we express our pain, and because it is so familiar, it becomes an important door through which we may discover our bigger self—and through this discovery, release our pain.

PAIN BODY

Some years ago on a commuter plane from Charlotte to Charlottesville I found myself sitting near a young couple with their toddler, and this young couple presented some vivid examples of pain body and pain speech. The young woman was very angry and disappointed with her partner because he did not acknowledge or respond to her, and she expressed this to him verbally through her pain speech in a high, emotional tone almost nonstop during the entire flight. The young man was probably as stressed out as she was, but instead of reacting with pain speech, he reacted with pain body: he held all of his stress inwardly and refused to respond, either in word or gesture. At one point he closed both his ears with his fingers—and when he did so, she finally stopped talking. But as soon as he released his ears, she started up again. Her speech was explosive and scattered; his body was closed and rigid. They were both experiencing similar pain, but as far as their awareness was concerned, both seemed totally disconnected from their true thoughts and feelings.

Some people are characterized more by pain body, others by pain speech, and still others by pain mind. The pain body is not just about the physical body. It can also be seen as the foundation, or ground, of our smaller unenlightened self, like a sense of identity. Think of someone who has been through many severe hardships in life but who has never managed to process the accompanying psychological, karmic, and emotional pain—the character played by Mickey Rourke in the film *The Wrestler* is a good example. Randy "The Ram" Robinson was once a star in the professional wrestling circuit, but when we meet him twenty years later, he is well past his prime, ailing with advanced heart disease and struggling to revive his identity as a wrestler. Randy spends a lot of his time in silence, seldom expressing any emotion. His ego is so dense that it almost manifests on a physical level: we can see the pain in his facial features, in his posture, in his measured way of moving, in his failing health. To loosen his dense identity, he medicates himself with alcohol and cocaine.

As the story progresses, Randy tries to rekindle a relationship with his estranged daughter. When the two meet, she touches his pain, and he begins to wake up a bit and to interact. As we observe this small awakening, we sense that this is a precious opportunity for Randy to connect not only with his daughter but also with a more genuine sense of self that can release his pain. But he is ultimately unable and unwilling to transform. He chooses instead to remain on his dead-end path; at the close of the film we are left with a feeling of deep sadness for him.

It is so important for the person characterized by the pain body to recognize the body through which the pain is flowing. Until one can discover the bounded, stuck self, there is no way to realize the deep, vast stillness that is free from pain: the aspect of oneself that is unconditioned and unbounded.

Pain Speech

To understand pain speech, think of someone you know who seems aways to be talking and talking but never has a point to make. This person does not realize that the pain itself is the one who is talking, and the pain becomes externalized in a scattered or confused way.

A classic example of pain speech is Frances McDormand's character Linda Litzke in the movie *Burn After Reading*. A fitness trainer in a health club, Linda is constantly explaining to everyone around her that she needs money for plastic surgery so she can attract the right man. She is so obsessed with verbalizing that she does not notice when her doting boss, who seems like the right man, says he cares deeply for her just as she is. She misses the opportunity to gain insight into the pain underlying her speech and through this recognition to find the feeling of connection she so clearly desires.

When you have an internal dialogue constantly running through your mind, this is another form of pain speech: the words go on and on, yet they never get you anywhere. Anyone characterized by pain speech can benefit from understanding that all these pain-based words are fruitless; for if you are not hearing your own words, why would you expect another to hear them? The first seed of doubt can help recognition to unfold: maybe what you are really trying to communicate is quite different from what you are expressing. With all her verbalizing, Linda might ultimately be saying that she felt hurt, unloved, and uncomfortable in herself.

When you start to connect more with the deeper truth at the source of pain speech, you can find the peaceful, pain-free place that is wordless, soundless, and where there is no expectation that someone must hear you. But first you must realize that your speech is an expression of pain—and the voice itself is what obscures the silence.

PAIN MIND

The person dominated by pain mind has too many scattered thoughts, too many emotions, too many mental images. Each time the mind moves to yet another emotion, thought, or image, that's what the mind becomes. When it doesn't move—when it gets stuck in one place—it becomes dense and dark, sometimes depressed.

Heath Ledger's character in *Brokeback Mountain* is an example of someone with pain mind. Ennis Del Mar is a troubled and troubling character, a man whose denial of his love for another man is causing him devastating psychic pain. His posture is rigid. He speaks very little, and when he does he speaks through a clamped jaw and barely gets his words out. He is trapped in his uncontrollable thoughts and emotions and spends a lifetime trying to deny them.

The pain mind is convinced it is achieving some purpose by all its activity and imagery. But if you look closer you can realize that all of these thoughts and emotions are mainly an expression of pain. This identification with thoughts is the small self, and in order to discover the big self you have to discover the small self. The pain itself becomes an entryway to self-discovery. The moment you catch yourself in a repetitive thought—for example, thinking over and over, "I hate the world"—in that moment you can realize "This is not me." In this moment of awareness, the pain begins to release, and something else is allowed to unfold. It is all a question of recognizing that moment.

The racing thoughts and emotions of pain mind—the infinite imaginings of the ego—have at their source the deep identification with pain known as pain body. Pain speech, too, arises from the pain body's mistaken sense of core identity. Thus, it is natural for a person to exhibit overlapping characteristics of pain body, pain speech, and pain mind—such as a tight jaw accompanied by churning thoughts. Ultimately, once we release ourselves from the pain body, then pain speech and pain mind will no longer be an issue. But sometimes the pain body is not clearly challenging us, whereas pain speech may be quite actively and obviously destroying our relationships, or pain mind may be immediately miring us in destructive thoughts or emotions and leading us to destructive actions. Our challenge is to identify the most advantageous place to begin the process of self-transformation.

Whether it is pain body, pain speech, or pain mind, moving past the small self is a matter of having some clue as to why you are doing, talking, or thinking as you are: deep inside you need a connection to your big self. Deep inside is your source of joy, but you go about searching for that joy in the wrong places and in the wrong activities of body, speech, and mind.

EFFORTLESS RESULT

Recently, one of my students in an online workshop wrote to me of a stressful encounter and of how it reminded her to connect to her deeper nature through her pain. She was meeting with the number-one-most-difficult person in her life to converse about her second-most-difficult person; but instead of reacting habitually, she instantly remembered her meditation practice and brought a sense of open awareness to the situation.

"For the first time ever, I just felt plenty of space and calmness surrounding every moment. And out of this space and calmness arose a tremendous warmth," she explained. She added that this simple moment of awareness helped her to gain confidence in her ability to dissolve the pain body and pain mind and access her deeper nature, while cultivating more compassion for others.

This example has an uplifting message for us: no matter how stuck we feel in our pain—regardless of our mental condition, no matter how confused we are or how strong our pride, ego, or fear—our more positive qualities are always accessible to us. The door to joy and peace of mind is always there.

That knowledge is a key thread throughout this book, and a key to all three doors. Everything and everyone has enlightened qualities, everything and everyone is perfect as they are. We already have a body of light. We already have the speech of the deity. Our mind already has the buddha nature, if we can only realize it.

In the midst of a challenging event, it is hard to see your own open, luminous nature, but it is there. Can you think back to an experience that at the time seemed like the most painful situation in your life yet turned out to be the greatest teaching, the greatest eye-opener, and to have given you the best direction of your life? Nearly all of us have had such an experience. During the Chinese Cultural Revolution so many Tibetan Buddhist and Bön monasteries and precious texts were destroyed, so many people died, so many people lost their country and went into exile; yet without this tragedy the precious teachings would not have been introduced to the rest of the world.

It is only when we look back later that we realize our difficult experience was the best thing that could have happened to us—and if not for the interference of our fears, we could have come to that realization even during the throes of the actual transition.

We don't see the perfection inherent in all major life transitions because we are so clouded by our uncertainties and insecurities. We fear an unknown future, and we fear losing the security and familiarity of the past. If Randy Robinson had been willing to give up his familiar world as a pro-wrestler and risk nurturing a genuine relationship with his daughter, he could have found the meaningful connection he so deeply craved. If Ennis Del Mar had risked an open relationship with his gay lover instead of choosing the safety and familiarity of conventional but empty marriage, he might have discovered a far richer and more fulfilling life.

Once you have moved through a difficult transition, there can be such a positive sense of freedom. You can discover that, no matter what happens, your physical world remains complete, your energy is strong, and your mind is at peace. Even if your external circumstances remain static, these feelings of peace and freedom are available to you if you can only find the doorway. When you feel stifled in marriage, divorce may not be necessary. When you are unsatisfied with your job, perhaps you don't need to quit to be happy and fulfilled.

It's like the story of an easy-going fellow relaxing in the desert who is approached by a successful businessman. The businessman asks him what he's up to, and the fellow responds, "Just relaxing and enjoying."

"You should find something to do," the businessman suggests.

"I don't have anything to do. I don't have a job."

"Well, then you should try to find some work," the businessman says. "Maybe I'll help you. You should learn some skills and get yourself a job. Then you'll learn more skills while on the job so you can find yourself a better job. Then someday maybe you'll get a higher-paid position like mine."

"And what then?" the idle fellow asks.

"Then, you will have money."

"Then what?"

"Then, you could enjoy the good life!"

The fellow says: "I'm already enjoying a good life! Why should I go to all that trouble to get to where I already am?"

In a way, this is what the dzogchen teachings tell us. The perfected qualities are already here, even before we strive to connect with them. They are in the base, they are in the path, and they are in the result. In the end, the higher experiences of body, speech, and mind come without effort.

DRAWING ATTENTION

People tend to search outside themselves for meaning and are drawn to what is foreign, different, or new, while what is already within tends to be ignored, denied, or misunderstood. My aim in writing this book, therefore, is to help you open your eyes and recognize what is always with you.

Your doorway to happiness, contentment, clarity, and wisdom is always with you. The point is to recognize that the door is there, generate a strong intention to enter through the door, and keep your attention focused in the right direction.

To gain knowledge of the doorway, read and study the wisdom teachings. Receive direct instruction from someone properly trained and knowledgeable in these teachings. Apply what you have learned in regular meditation practice. It is called "practice" because we are practicing something. We are not already illuminated, and our work will not necessarily be easy. In every practice, minimum, medium or maximum effort will be involved.

Then, make an effort to recall what you have learned. You don't need to be reminded to feel depressed when the alarm sounds on a Monday morning. You don't need to be reminded to worry, fret, judge someone, or get angry at them. But when your painful emotions, thoughts, memories, and senses do arise and intensify, they can also spark a recollection that they can be used either as an exit from, or as an entrance into, the nature of mind. They can remind you to practice, using whatever method you can most skillfully apply.

Remembering the doorway of body, speech, or mind is not enough; you must also generate a strong intention to enter it. Prayer can be very helpful in strengthening and activating your intention.

Importantly, you must draw your attention in the right direction. You can discover what is on the other side of the door: your essence is there. But first you need to know it's there and then draw your attention toward it and away from your emotions, busy thoughts, or other distractions.

Attention is important because it is the support of awareness. For example, I may be taking a pleasant walk through the park and then suddenly think of a person I don't like. I refer to this as my "famous person": the one who pushes all my buttons, the person whose image alone is enough to propel me into a full manifestation of pain body, pain speech, or pain mind. Unless I am able to move my focus away from my famous person, I will find it difficult to let go of my racing thoughts or emotions related to that person.

If the mental image of this person calls up anger, for example, I can try diverting my attention outward to the beauty of the park, engaging with that beauty and feeling joy in it. Or I can bring my attention inward to my heart, allow myself to feel the spontaneous presence of love there and engage with the quality of love. Alternatively, in a more spiritual sense, I can take some time to visualize above me the presence of my root teacher as the embodiment of all the buddhas and bodhisattvas, cultivate a pure connection to his wisdom and his blessings, and through attention and awareness engage in those enlightened qualities.

Even visualizing my teacher relies on imagery. If I divert my focus to *who* is experiencing the anger, I am looking at the true source of the anger. This is the highest way to draw attention to the essence. When I observe the anger without analyzing or judging and then observe the observer in the same way, both observer and observed dissolve spontaneously into their clear, luminous nature. Pain body dissolves into stillness, pain speech dissolves into silence, pain mind dissolves into the spaciousness of pure nonconceptual awareness.

The source of anger and any other negative emotion is the same base from which all experiences of samsara and nirvana arise. Because negative emotions arise from the same place that nirvana arises from, they can serve as a door.

CHOOSING THE RIGHT DOOR

In the pages to come, I offer a wide variety of teachings and practices related to body, speech, and mind, everything from a discussion of how one achieves the body of light—the highest attainment of dzogchen practice—to mantras that provide healing through sound, to energy practices that enhance clarity of mind in meditation practice. All of this information is based on ancient teachings, and I have tried to present it in the most accessible way possible while still staying faithful to each original source.

For me, the ancient texts are important, and I always present the teachings from that point of view. Yet I find that people relate better and come to a more direct experience of the deeper truths when I bring the teachings down to earth in a very concrete way that makes sense to our modern Western lives. Every teaching that is given should be directly related to the mind that is the object of liberation. When the teachings are understood and touch people's hearts and lives, that is what is really helpful in the end. Those who are ready for more in-depth study and practice will be able to find their way from there. I recommend reading the entire book since many of these wisdom teachings mesh with and complement the understanding of the others.

Which door do you choose at any given time—body, speech, or mind? If your most disturbing problem is physical or if you find yourself relating primarily through the pain body, it may be best to choose a practice related to the body. If your pain is more energy- or speech-related, then the practices of speech, sound, or energy may be best. (Speech is more closely related to energy, or *prana*, than it is to the body or mind.) Disturbances of the mind respond well to practices that emphasize work with the mind.

It is not that the door of the body is related only to our physical experience, or the door of the mind only to the dimension of mind. Body, speech, and mind all are related. What happens outside us affects what happens within and vice versa. For example, someone whose business is failing may be susceptible to stress-related physical illness. Being physically ill can make one vulnerable to emotional difficulties, and uncontrolled emotions can cloud the mind. I remember a fellow monk in India who developed a bad cough and became convinced he had tuberculosis. In time he developed a limp and needed a walking stick. But as soon as he got his test results and found he was healthy after all, he threw away the walking stick. Sickness can be completely wrapped up in one's state of mind.

Words also have powerful effects on us mentally, energetically, and physically. A chronically ill person who says with conviction, "I don't want to die," may actually be able to lengthen his or her life through the force of willpower.

As the pages to come will reveal, having an understanding of the connection between body, speech, and mind can significantly enhance our ability to progress in spiritual practice. However, there is a difference between knowing about this connection and actually applying it. For example, I've known of many devoted yoga practitioners who focus on the physical effects of yoga—how good it makes them look and feel—without having any notion of how the yoga postures and breathing techniques can serve toward achieving a higher realization of their consciousness. On the other hand, there are yogis accomplished in higher meditations of the mind and prana who neglect the physical dimension of their practice.

Practitioners who understand these subtle interactions of body, speech, and mind are much more likely to succeed in achieving the ultimate goal of self-realization.

Part 1

Eternal Body
gyurwa mépé ku

Introduction to Body 1

A FEW DAYS before his death, one of my childhood teachers, Gen Singtrug, could be found working away at a sewing machine in the monastery. I remember watching him from the next room, the beautiful afternoon light streaming in on his frail form through the window as he was singing the songs he loved and stitching together the banners that were to be burned with his body when he was cremated.

Gen Singtrug could be said to personify the subtlest form of body known as *eternal body*. Imagine that, like Gen Singtrug, you can experience a continual sense of youthful playfulness and innocence with no interference from your physical body even as it goes through aging, pain, sickness, or the dying process. This sense of eternal youth is related to one's essence and is itself a kind of body, an entity that supports your sense of who you are, the experience of your being.

Throughout life one's physical body is subject to constant change. Yet one's essence never changes. This is what is meant by *eternal body*. In its highest sense the body is pure, like the dharmakaya, like pure emptiness or pure space. According to the dzogchen teachings, we all have a connection to that essence through our bodies.

EMPOWERING THE BODY

Even from our place in the pain body—that familiar, dense sense of egoistic identity formed by our conceptual, karmic, and emotional conditions—at any time we can find our way to a lighter sense of body.

Sitting in meditation is one method. Another is simply the way we attend to our physical body and our physical environment.

In the Bön shamanic tradition, one approach to physical empowerment is to wear sacred objects on your body. A red or blue robe, a red or white hat, a turquoise stone around the neck or a mala (Tibetan rosary) around the wrist can remind practitioners of their more enlightened qualities.

Just taking a shower and dressing in a way that makes you feel good can be empowering. How you look is not essentially important—some people already feel so peaceful and comfortable in themselves that they have no need to rely much on their appearance. But most of us have been conditioned from an early age to feel that appearance is important. When the conditions of our physical appearance affect us, we need to pay attention.

By adjusting our physical circumstances, we are able to create an energetic dimension that supports the higher experiences of the mind and thus can be considered a kind of body. We can clean our house, decorate it with flowers, and add attractive lighting. We can add precious images and objects of devotion to our meditation area for another level of effect. The higher experiences of mind do not necessarily depend on our creating the right environment and the right energetic dimension, but they are supported by doing so. If I'm trying to awaken more joy in myself, I will have a harder time achieving it if I rely only on my mind. By decorating my house, I'm already creating a different level of energy and seeing myself differently.

In the sutra tradition of both Bön and Buddhism, right actions of body and speech are strongly emphasized, in part because these grosser levels of activity are easier to control than one's mind. When you go window-shopping, consider how difficult it is to stop your mind from mentally making purchases. Compare the number of these "purchases" to the far fewer number of "purchases" your speech makes by responding "yes" when the salesperson asks if he or she can help you, and the still fewer "purchases" your body makes by actually trying on some items in the dressing room.

Monks who take the *vinaya* vows of the sutra tradition commit to refrain from lying, stealing, killing, using drugs or alcohol, or engaging in harmful sexual behavior or other nonvirtuous activities of body and speech. Yet it is said that breaking a vinaya vow is like breaking a clay pot: it is very difficult to restore the vow afterward. Breaking a vow of tantra, on the other hand, is said to be like breaking a gold pot. Tantra emphasizes vows of the mind: they are easier to restore because, like gold, the mind is malleable and never loses its value.

Tantra is known as the path of transformation. Despite its emphasis on mind, through visualization practices, tantra offers a profound level of physical empowerment. In the ancient Tibetan Bön teachings of tantra, the body itself is seen as a palace of the divine, as a fundamental aspect of enlightenment. The divine abides as space and light in every distinct energy function of your body. Every cell, every sense organ, every internal organ is associated with a deity. Not only does blood flow through your veins, carrying oxygen and vital nutrients to all your cells, but the body also contains sacred winds of energy flowing through sacred channels of light, bearing luminous spheres of awareness through all of your experience.

During tantric meditation one may visualize transforming into an enlightened deity such as the Buddha of Compassion or a loving goddess such as Tara or (in the Bön tradition) Shérap Chamma. The moment you feel such a transformation taking place, your self-image can change from that of a weak, angry person, heavy with ego, to that of a spacious, light-filled being who fully embodies the pure qualities of love and compassion.

The White Liquid Practice to Heal Disease (see chapter 4) is another example of a tantric practice. Keep in mind, during visualization practice, it is important for the tantric practitioner to recognize, experience, and emphasize an actual shift in the physical dimension. You can draw special attention to changes that are felt in your flesh, blood, skin, bones, and internal organs—in every cell in your body. At the same time, you can bring a little more awareness to your body's connection with a deity's specific qualities. For example, when practitioners transform into Shenlha Ökar (Shen Deity of White Light), they visualize their bodies as being adorned with the thirteen ornaments of peacefulness that in themselves evoke the enlightened quality of peace-fulness.[2] Shenlha Ökar himself embodies all six of the antidote qualities of love, generosity, wisdom, openness, peacefulness, and compassion; so as soon as you transform into Shenlha Ökar, you instantly embody these same qualities.

This type of subtle shift in the physical dimension is an important element of the practice. Your body image has so much to do with your normal sense of identity. It affects your confidence, your mood, and how you relate to yourself and to your environment. Once you have formed a specific image of your physical appearance—whether you see yourself as too fat, too thin, too tall, or too old—you become conditioned by that image, and the image may become an obstacle to your open awareness. When you are less conditioned by the physical or energetic aspects of the body and more by its mind aspect, you can connect more easily with your inner wisdom and with your more enlightened qualities.

FINDING STILLNESS

One of the closest experiences you can have through your body of self-realization is when you are able to reach a deep place of stillness, like the stillness of a mountain. Being in this deep place of stillness can be no different from abiding in the inseparable state of the essence and nature of mind.

Exhaustion can bring you to this kind of stillness. After working a long, hard day of physical labor, you arrive home feeling utterly depleted, fall back into a comfortable chair, and relax fully into that sense of stillness. The body is still, the speech is still, the mind is still. There is a deep sense of release, of connection, of completion, of whole-ness. This is a clear example of how the pain body itself may be used as a doorway.

Without practice, this experience of stillness will remain only until a distracting movement occurs. Even a simple hand gesture can lead to a loss of connection, drawing your mind back into its habitual patterns.

2. See chapter 13, "The Divine Being of Light."

The distraction comes not from the movement but from your relation to the movement. This is the point of regular meditation practice—even when your body is not literally exhausted, through meditation you can bring yourself to that same deep place of release. You can relax into the stillness, abide in it, familiarize yourself with it, and over time stabilize it. Once the experience is fully stabilized, no physical movement will disturb it.

There is a specific dzogchen meditation practice in which we bring ourselves to the place of stillness by closing the eyes and contemplating all of the body's physical actions over a lifetime, action by action, day by day, year by year. Although we can't review our entire life in a single meditation session, we can elicit enough physical memories to bring ourselves to the point of exhaustion. The instant we arrive at this point, we release all the actions into the stillness of the moment and abide without changing. "Abide without changing" means that as our thoughts and experiences continue to arise and dissolve, we continue to rest in our own nature and simply observe without elaborating. We try not to follow the past, plan the future, or change the present. We "leave it as it is."

This type of exhaustion practice is not limited to the body; it can be used also with the speech and with the mind. One reflects on a lifetime of speech, then releases all the speech into the silence—a deep silence, like the silence of someone who has awakened from a dream and has no words to describe it. With the mind practice, one contemplates all the thinking one has done over a lifetime and on arriving at the place of exhaustion, one releases all the thoughts into the space of pure, thought-free awareness, like a clear sky.

The stillness of the body, the silence of speech, and the spacious awareness of mind are the true three doors to enlightenment. Ultimately, one aims to connect with, appreciate, and rest in the fullness and pure potentiality of the nature of mind.

DOORWAYS TO SELF-REALIZATION

The coming chapter, on the three bodies, will provide a precise understanding of how you experience your self-image through the body;

how this self-image evolves as your spiritual practice matures; and importantly, how you can effectively work with this knowledge at key stages. Next, chapter 3, on the body of light—the highest attainment of dzogchen practice—will reveal how your conditioned body originally developed from pure space and light and how you can reverse this process in order to begin to connect with your true nature as a being of light. Chapter 4 will offer guided instructions for the practice of the five-point meditation posture, the White Liquid Practice to Heal Disease, Tibetan yoga, and prostrations. The main thread throughout all of these teachings and practices is that your self-image is not only influenced by your physical conditions, it is also a product of your karma and your thought patterns. Through knowledge and through regular meditation practice, you have the power to transform your self-image, your sense of identity, and your life.

As Gen Singtrug showed us at his sewing machine, even at the time of death, the worst physical condition you can possibly experience, the body still offers a doorway to the divine, to your essence. Most of us will not assume a seated meditation posture or do complicated breathing exercises while we are taking our last breath. But we can still meditate and connect through the experience of our physical body to our nonphysical, eternal body.

A student of mine once shared with me a moving and inspiring example of using physical illness as a door. A few months before his death in 2004, Ron Langman sent me the following letter to share with the *sangha*, or community of practitioners. Ron describes his experiences with guru yoga, a meditation practice that enables one to connect deeply with the essence of the spiritual master.

> Since 1980 I have tried to gain some experience in medita-
> tion. I studied with Geshé Gudun Lodro, who taught me the
> practices of calm abiding and guru yoga. In twenty years my
> meditations were uneven, unexceptional, and frenetic. Off
> in worldly concerns, fantasies, indolence, and pride—that's
> how it was.
>
> Last year my brain tumor flared up, and I had to have
> surgery to remove part of my brain and the tumor. The doc-

tors wanted me awake so they could ask me to do things during surgery in order to gauge how much good brain they were removing. This was a long and arduous experience. As the surgery progressed, I started doing guru yoga with Lama Tenzin as my object of refuge. I repeated from the bardo teaching, "Lama, from your compassion, bless me," and focused my mind on his image. As time drew on, Lama Tenzin appeared as a great golden being, and the Tibetan syllable *A* began to come out of his body to me. I felt loved not only by Lama Tenzin but by the whole sangha. It got me through the surgery.

So by this illness and great trauma, guru yoga appeared to me in a powerful way. It has become true for me that moments of great suffering or fear can also become moments of great devotion and faith. I share this example with the sangha in the hope that merit will come to us all to help sentient beings in as many ways as possible.[3]

Even in his terrible physical condition, Ron was still able to maintain his connection and his virtue. His fear and the emotions brought on by his physical pain and suffering were the door.

3. Edited lightly for clarity and reprinted with permission of Linda Langman, Ron's wife.

The Three Bodies 2

I LIVED IN Italy some years ago and used to walk past the same old man day after day. From the way he held himself as he sat on the park bench, always hunched over and motionless, I could tell he was sitting on a lot of mental, energetic, and physical traces—perhaps from his experiences in the war or from a long-gone career—with no clear way to process what had happened in his life.

You often can read the bodies of people around you. Try looking at any driver next to you on the road on a Monday morning and you may see all the expectations and distracted thoughts of a Monday morning reflected in the way the driver holds his or her head, stares at the road, and grips the wheel. The striking qualities of the commuter and of the old man in the park are so different from the quality we would see in a person heading home from work on a Friday afternoon and different still from the quality of a person sitting on a mountaintop in deep meditation—spine straight, chest open, eyes gazing at the sky, abiding in the nature of mind.

The reality is, your body is far more than the image you see in the mirror or the sensation of fullness you have after a good meal. Beyond its purely physical nature, the body can be seen as both a reflection and the source of your entire range of experience, including your spiritual realization.

This broader view of the body forms the basis of a full set of teachings by the eighth-century Bön master Nangzher Lopo. Nangzher Lopo was one of the great masters of the *Oral Transmission of Zhang Zhung*

(*Zhang Zhung Nyen Gyü*), one of the most revered series of Bön dzog-chen teachings, and he was one of the main disciples of Tapihritsa, a prominent master who achieved the rainbow body at the end of his life. Nangzher Lopo gave his teaching on the three bodies to a master named Phowa Gyelzig Sechung.

Nangzher Lopo explained that, at any given time, each of us experiences through one of three different types of body: the *conceptual karmic body*, the *illusory wisdom body*, or the *changeless precious body*. Knowing which one of these three we embody reveals the doorways to the higher bodies. His teachings tell us:

> the right eye to see through
> the right teachings to seek
> the right practices to do
> the right experiences to cultivate
> the right view in which to gain confidence.

Nangzher Lopo's teachings can empower your meditation practice. They also reveal a new way of looking at yourself. If you're not happy with your current physical body, you can't give birth to a new one, yet you can always give birth to a new mind, and with it a new sense of body. No matter what you've been through—whether addiction, abandonment, or abuse—you have the power to recreate yourself.

THE CONCEPTUAL KARMIC BODY

The old man in the park and the Monday morning commuter both might be said to inhabit the conceptual karmic body (*namtok barlé gyi lü*), the first body defined by Nangzher Lopo. This category can also be said to comprise the pain body. It reflects the normal samsaric view, the view supported by the consensus reality surrounding us—what we see on television, what we've learned in school, what our parents taught us.

The conceptual karmic body has a heaviness and a denseness. It is problematic since its dualistic view and habit of clinging to things as if they are permanent and unchanging tend to produce a lot of suffering, desire, and intolerance. Our experience of this body has much to do with our personal sense of identity. And that identity is wrapped up in our feelings, our sense of boundaries, our belief system, and our personal vision of ourselves and the world around us.

As human beings, we all share a similar experience of the conceptual karmic body because we all are born under the same set of basic human conditions. These conditions are what make us find joy in drinking a cup of tea or coffee, for example, or in listening to music or walking on the beach. Compare our sense of identity as humans to that of a hawk, who because of having a different type of conceptual karmic body, finds value in a rising column of warm air, or to that of a gold-fish who delights in a floating breadcrumb but can see no pleasure in a deep breath of fresh air.

Yet, two individual human beings also have two very different experiences of the conceptual karmic body. Even if they live in the same house, in the same neighborhood of the same city, attend the same school, and work the same job, one might feel he is living in a hell realm and the other might feel he is living in the heaven realm. This is because nearly everything we know about what is good or bad, right or wrong, pleasant or unpleasant, we learn after birth from our unique personal experiences. Our cultural and family upbringing, our religious training, along with all our personal encounters and physical and emotional sensitivities, contribute to shaping our hopes, fears, perspectives, and sense of self.

To achieve true self-realization, you must ultimately shed the conceptual, dualistic view that you have cultivated over a lifetime. Yet, as Nangzher Lopo points out, until you can let go of that view, the conceptual karmic body remains very useful as a doorway to liberation. For without this first body, you would be unable to understand and reflect on the teachings or engage in meditation practice, and wisdom could not arise in you. The ability to exercise your intellect is helpful for achieving the higher experiences of body—and ultimately, toward gaining final liberation from the cycle of death and rebirth. In the end, the liberation of the body is the liberation of one's self.

THE ILLUSORY WISDOM BODY

Through the teachings, the introduction by the master, the practice, and the blessings, you can gradually deconstruct and dissolve the karmic conceptual body and be introduced to another type of body and identity called the illusory wisdom body (*yeshé gyumé lü*). This second body is characterized by wisdom—realization of the truth—and by a positive sense of the illusory.

Someone who has the illusory wisdom body realizes the ultimate truth that nothing has any existence in and of itself. Everything he or she experiences is transient, dependently related, subject to conditions, and thus empty of any defining essence. This experience is like watching a magic act when you already know all the sleight of hand behind it. While the rest of the audience around you is completely taken in—amazed to see a live rabbit pulled from a hat, shocked to see a woman locked in a trunk and stabbed by swords—you know everything is illusion and have no fear. For the illusory wisdom body, all vision—meaning all thoughts, mental images, emotions, sensory experiences, and so forth—is experienced as a projection of the mind, like a rainbow or an echo, with no real substance.

When you can internalize this deeper truth and really embody it, you no longer struggle with your experiences. You become more clear, lucid, open, and free—free of your own conceptual ideas, free of hatred and grasping. As this sense of realization reaches more subtle levels, you can experience even more spaciousness and freedom. Because you are less rigid and blocked, you flow through each moment. The denser sense of identity that is the basis of your pain in samsara becomes lighter and more transparent, and you have a clearer sense of yourself and the world around you as illusion.

There is also increased spontaneity, humor, and joy. Your sense of happiness is less dependent on what you have than on who you are. What you have can change in an instant, but if your happiness stems from your connection with the self that never changes, this is called realization. You are not denying your conventional experience of reality, but you are not blindly dependent on that experience either.

Consider that everything you possess at this moment is, by its very nature, guaranteed not to be yours. Sooner or later, every relationship you have is guaranteed to dissolve. Everything that lives will die; everything that is created eventually will be destroyed. If impermanence is the true nature of reality, this is all the more reason not to get too attached to your visions. People who feel a little more open are sensing indirectly or directly that this is the case. People who feel blocked are, indirectly, not realizing impermanence. They think they can hold on forever to relationships and possessions, yet everything they are trying so hard to grasp is only an illusion.

THE CHANGELESS PRECIOUS BODY

When one has unwavering confidence in the realization of the second body, one achieves the third body, the changeless precious body (*gyurwa mépa rinpoché lü*). Unlike the conceptual karmic body and the illusory wisdom body, the changeless precious body is not a process, it is the result. It *is* the inseparable state of essence and nature. To have realization of the truth and have total confidence in it is the ultimate body.

Just as the truth itself is changeless, your deeper experiences of the truth will also be changeless. With the third body, what you have achieved does not change. In every moment, whatever experiences, emotions, or thoughts arise are spontaneously released without grasping or aversion. They continuously self-liberate, like snowflakes falling in the ocean.

You can experience a glimpse of this third body at moments of exhaustion, such as during the dzogchen exhaustion practice previously mentioned. When you release all your effort, emotions, and thoughts, a door may open for you to experience another dimension, another space, and other qualities. You may begin to feel more free, light, joyful, and energetic, with a new sense of potential. Imagine what it would feel like to win a mega-million dollar lottery—if your car suddenly breaks down or if your computer is stolen, you will still feel fine. Nothing can change your experience. You are resting in a sense of victory and release and you feel changeless.

The experience of changelessness becomes stabilized only through practice. Stability involves being grounded, connected, and confident in the realization of your deepest nature. When you achieve the changeless precious body, you become fearless. Being afraid nearly always has to do with fear of change; but now, change no longer brings fear of loss or fear of having something you don't want. Experiences will always come and go, but the one who experiences never does. You cannot lose your self, so there is no fear of losing anything.

FINDING LIBERATION THROUGH THE THREE BODIES

As your capacity changes over time, you may find that these different bodies will manifest, perhaps one more often than another. Whatever body you find yourself in at a given moment, you can draw on Nang-zher Lopo's teachings to help transform your experience.

The Three Eyes

Each of the three bodies has a type of eye, or capacity for perception. It's easy to understand how different people can see from very different perspectives. Imagine a house by the side of the road: a person with the eye of a realtor may immediately visualize a "for sale" sign out front; someone with a photographer's eye may see the house as a framed image; the house's owner may notice only the peeling paint; the next-door neighbor may see only how much larger the house is than his own.

The eye that is needed to overcome the conceptual karmic body can be developed only through study and knowledge. It is the wisdom eye (*shérab gyi chen*)—the eye that offers the ability to perceive, reflect on, and have some conceptual understanding of the dharma. The wisdom eye cuts the root of samsara and allows you to see the truth of the conceptual body. If there is no wisdom eye, you will not understand the truth, enter on the right path, attain the illusory wisdom body, or ultimately achieve liberation.

For someone who already has the illusory wisdom body, the eye of bön (*bön gyi chenma*) is needed in order to attain the changeless precious body. The eye of bön is essentially a capacity for remembering or awakening to the teachings when the need arises. If you have the eye of bön and something disturbing happens, instead of awakening to anger and a memory of what some hateful person has done to you, you will spontaneously remember the master, the teaching, or the practices. This insight arises in the illusory wisdom body when the mind is not particularly focused on attaining something. The moment you relax and release your goals and desires, the eye of bön naturally opens and the energy flows.

The changeless precious body needs the eye of omniconsciousness (*namba thamjé khyenpé chenma*). This last eye sees the infinite nature of space. Without the eye of omniconsciousness, you are like a blind bird continually searching for the end of the sky—your conceptual mind can never find the truth because it is blind to it. Your wisdom remains subject to conditions, your realization is limited, and your awareness is interrupted when the meditation session ends.

When you have the eye of omniconsciousness, you see the truth that is beyond concepts. The words of your teacher no longer matter; nor do your thoughts or knowledge or the message of the scriptures. Everything is complete. All searching for realization is ended and no more contradiction or conflict exists in your mind. Primordial awareness is totally merged with the essence, or base of all. You experience naked awareness, pure presence, changeless essence, the state without a base, beyond hope and fear, beyond confinement and liberation, with no need for action and no need to change or to grasp.

This is the realization of the sky. There is no interruption or obscuration. The clouds of conceptual thoughts and emotions can obscure your perception, but the sky itself is not obscured.

The Three Truths

Because each of the three bodies has a different view of the truth, each benefits from a different form of teaching. Therefore, knowing which body you are in can help you to know the most beneficial form of teaching for your needs.

The conceptual karmic body finds its truth in external actions and events, and in concepts, emotions, and relationships. Just as a person who is starving might experience a piece of bread as the highest truth and yet perceive no value at all in the wisdom of emptiness, someone with the conceptual karmic body will find teachings of speech most effective and will perhaps find more value in those teachings than in being in the presence of the actual Buddha.

For someone who achieves the illusory wisdom body, truth is no longer primarily found externally; rather, it is found everywhere. It is experienced in space, in stillness, in simply being. The happiness of the blessings can be felt in the presence of the master, a friend, an image, or light. For the illusory wisdom body, being in the physical presence of the teacher is more empowering than the words the teacher uses.

The experience of the truth for the changeless precious body is that everything is already naturally pure and perfected. The heart/mind connection with the teacher and teachings is very strong and is not changed or interrupted by time or space; it depends neither on the presence nor the words of the teacher. When someone is prepared for heart and mind transmission, the connection, the ability to receive, is just there.

Another way to understand the experience of each of these three truths is to imagine sitting on a favorite "cushion." Think of those moments when you have free time with nothing to distract you. You unconsciously look for an invisible cushion to rest on. Sometimes you may choose a cushion that brings an immediate feeling of familiarity that is not necessarily good for you but is comforting. Other times, you may find yourself planted on a cushion where you don't necessarily care to be sitting. Your conceptual karmic cushion may be rather old, tattered, and stale smelling; your illusory wisdom cushion may appear fresh and bright.

These teachings of Nangzher Lopo help us to recognize how many old, tattered cushions we have and how many that are fresh and clear. In order to have a spacious, luminous view you must perceive from your place on the spacious, luminous cushion. Someone who has the changeless precious experience will abide in the nature of mind on the dharmakaya cushion, where nothing changes. It is a matter of recognizing the different cushions, familiarizing yourself with the more beneficial ones, and stabilizing the experience.

The Three Knowledges

For each of the three bodies there is a type of knowledge that can liberate you from that body.

If you have a karmic conceptual body, you tend to look outward for the truth. As you are looking out, Nangzher Lopo suggests trying to allow clear, thought-free knowledge to arise. Let your consciousness become mirrorlike and externally all will appear clear and empty like a reflection in the mirror. A mirror does not grasp the images reflected in it; all the images self-arise, self-abide, and self-liberate.

During contemplation or meditation you can close your eyes and imagine your heart as a mirror. When you open your eyes, experience that they are a direct, transparent entryway to your heart and that everything you see outside of you is a reflection. If you can do this, everything you see will support your clarity of heart/mind in the same way that the clarity of an image reflected in a mirror directly supports your experience of the mirror's clarity.

As the illusory wisdom body manifests over time, your focus will begin to turn inward. You will be more connected to your self and less dependent on outer circumstances. The practice for the illusory wisdom body, therefore, involves looking inward: observe each thought and emotion as it arises and as it spontaneously dissolves. The experience will be clear and thought-free.

To cultivate the recognition of this empty awareness within you, imagine a lamp shining within a crystal vase. Within the vase there is both space (emptiness) and light (awareness), and these two aspects are inseparable. This is the knowledge that liberates from the illusory wisdom body.

When the two experiences of emptiness and awareness dissolve into each other as an unchanging experience of open awareness, external and internal space are unified. Your wisdom no longer looks outward or inward and the wisdom is said to be hidden like lightning in a daytime sky. This is the liberation of the changeless precious body. It is the deepest form of bliss and joy, free of the activities of the conceptual mind and of the views of nihilism or eternalism.[4]

---

4. When your grasping mind perceives subject and object as having inherent existence, that is the extreme of eternalism. If in searching for subject and object you do not find anything and therefore conclude that nothing exists, that is the extreme of nihilism.

TABLE 2.1. THE THREE BODIES

Three bodies	Three eyes	Three truths	Three knowledges	Three experiences	Three confidences
Conceptual karmic body	Wisdom eye	Vision of delusion Nirmanakaya Speech teachings	Extroverted wisdom What you see externally is clear and thought free *Example*: mirror image *Advice*: Liberate without being trapped by methods	All internal and external phenomena seem clear, pure, unpre-dictable, and unconditioned Dharmakaya vision arises	Thingless, ceaseless qualities
Illusory wisdom body	Eye of bön	Vision of bön essence Sambhogakaya Body teachings	Introverted wisdom Experience is clear and thought free *Example*: inter-nally aware and empty, like a lamp in a vase *Advice*: Overcome all hope and fear	One sees all unceas-ingly, without thoughts, clear without grasping The vision of bön essence arises	Empty, clear qualities
Changeless precious body	Eye of omni-conscious-ness	Naturally pure vision Dharmakaya Mind teachings	Hidden wisdom Primordial wis-dom is dissolved into the inner space; external and internal space are unified *Example*: sacredly blissful and empty, like light in the sky at dawn *Advice*: Go beyond eternalism and nihilism	The unob-scured wis-dom clearly arises; without renouncing, the ignorance dissolves Buddha vision arises	Infinite, perfected qualities

Source: Nangzher Lopo's teaching from the *Nyen Gyü* experiential transmission

The Three Experiences

Nangzher Lopo further describes the unique experiences one will have when the different bodies dissolve.

When the conceptual body dissolves, all appearances produced by the conceptual mind—all the ideas, feelings, and realities that seem so solid to you—also dissolve effortlessly, and you have the experience of openness and emptiness. All appearances arise unpredictably, and they clear by themselves. Everything flows. You are no longer searching for anything, yet everything is present. The dharmakaya vision arises.

As the illusory wisdom body dissolves, you have the experience of potentiality and clarity, of omniconsciousness that is unceasing. Whatever appearances arise, you are fully with them and with their essence. The vision of bön essence and of the sambhogakaya arises.

The dissolution of the changeless precious body brings the bliss of manifestation, of the nirmanakaya, which arises from the inseparability of clarity and emptiness. When clear, ceaseless, unobscured wisdom arises, ignorance dissipates effortlessly without any need to renounce, purify, or tame it. In that awakening, everything is perfected and buddha vision arises. All phenomena and all beings are seen as enlightened; all forms are seen as light; all beings are seen as pure beings. This is the final liberation.

The Three Confidences

In order to seal the results of each body's dissolution, you must have confidence in a particular view. Confidence in this case is not likened to trust in a certain outcome—as in "I'm confident I will not get sick," or "I'm confident you will repay my loan with interest." That kind of confidence is strongly related to one's expectations. Rather, confidence in a view has more to do with confidence in being open to the outcome, whatever that outcome might be: "If I'm meant to be healed, it's fine. If I'm not meant to be healed, it's fine too." Confidence in a view is similar to confidence in space.

Thomas Edison had some confidence in space when he was searching for a filament for the light bulb. He tried thousands of different materials until he found one that succeeded, but he explained that he never considered any of these attempts as failures; instead, they were each an opportunity to learn what didn't work. Having that much openness, with the energy and willingness to make every mistake possible in the process—that is a higher sense of confidence that I find is often lacking in students of the dharma.

The normal attitude would be that you have to chase after a result. But meditation practice is not a question of chasing after something: if you open your eyes, you will see there is so much that life already is giving you. In my own experience, I have learned to sit and abide in that sense of openness in myself. It is such a simple act, yet it has so much meaning in the Bön tradition, for my teachers and for myself. The experience of sitting and abiding is like encountering a god if you will—the purest, formless form of the divine before the divine appears with the qualities and form of a deity. If it's so beautiful to hear some-one bring form to their love by expressing it, it is even more beautiful to connect with the state from which that expression arises. The pure quality of that formless state is alive, vivid. It is the origin, the mother's womb, the source of wisdom. For me personally, that is what it is.

When you abide in openness, you are connecting to the source. When you are unable to abide, it is because your mind is elaborating. Elabo-rating on clarity obscures rigpa, the innate awareness. Elaborating on openness, or emptiness, obscures the base. When the base is obscured, the pure quality of love or joy cannot arise from it. If you are diagnosed with the samsaric disease of ignorance, then the prescription is to abide in that space. It is not only a question of recognizing the space, but also of familiarizing yourself with it and integrating this experience into everyday life. This is how one cultivates confidence in the view.

To be liberated from the karmic conceptual body, one must gain confidence in the view of emptiness. There is more luminosity and potentiality in space than there is within the things and activities that arise within space, but the only way to discover spacious luminosity is to minimize the fear that one will lose the light as a result of losing things. In a way, we are so conditioned by the luminosity we experience in things that we have almost no trust in the existence of light in space itself. In the first body it is very important to let go of the experiences and conditions we have been holding onto in order to fully experience our connection with the space within.

To be liberated from the illusory wisdom body, one needs to gain confidence in the view of the inseparable state of clarity and emptiness. The closer your connection is with the space, the more potential you will experience within the space, and you will find that the whole light of the universe exists in the space within you.

To be liberated from the changeless precious body, one must have confidence in the view that everything is perfected beyond all qualities and conditions.

THE THREE BODIES IN DAILY LIFE

Some of these ideas may sound overly esoteric to people who are new to Tibetan Buddhist or Bön Buddhist principles. Yet, not only meditation practice but also daily life can offer many opportunities to become familiar with the experiences described above. Consider that in every process of loss, there is first darkness and sadness, and then there is light. That is true, whether in the death of a family member, the loss of a job, or even at a time of tears or sexual climax. Just letting out a deep breath can be a doorway to a deep experience of meditation: breathe in deeply, then release—all experience is complete in that very moment.

We have so much fear of loss, yet these moments of loss give us an opportunity to experience the absence of our conditions, to experience the clarity within the space, and to realize that everything is already perfected. The closer our connection is with the space, the more potentiality we can experience within the space.

I find it interesting when people say that a difficult experience has helped them to know themselves better. What this usually means is that they have come to identify even more strongly with their conditions and have established and reinforced their pain body as their samsaric identity. Other people find themselves in limbo after a loss because they continue clinging to what they have lost and they never experience completion. The right experience of closeness to one's self comes not from connecting with one's conditions but from connecting with the loss of one's conditions. That very point where you start to feel like you are losing something and have no control over it can be the biggest moment of discovery. Everything that you thought you needed, you don't need. You are complete. The moment you glimpse that completion you can discover the aliveness, the joyful potentiality, the ceaseless quality.

It is a question of having confidence in that experience. To develop confidence, one must take every opportunity to be more accepting of the circumstances of loss, connect with the space, and trust that the space is the place where love and light will manifest—and it is.

The space that opens up is really about freedom. All the small freedoms we experience in our life give access to the biggest, most powerful freedom, like rivers running into the sea.

The Body of Light: 3
The Final Result of Dzogchen Practice

S PACE AND LIGHT play a prominent role in all of dzogchen practice, and never more so than during the final liberation of a great dzogchen master. At the time of death, the best practitioners are the ones who achieve the third body, the changeless precious body, and are able to enter the natural state in its naked aspect without distraction. As they are freed from their physical body, they are ready to complete the knowledge and qualities of the Buddha's body, speech, and mind. They can then act ceaselessly to help sentient beings. Even more accomplished are the ones who do not even need to die. Instead of dying and decomposing, the body dissolves into the boundless space of the natural state, and the practitioner assumes the rainbow body, or body of light.

Just as the three bodies are each experienced through your own physical body, the body of light also has to do with the physical body in its purest state. How is it possible for the gross physical body to dissolve into pure light and space? It can do so because light and space already exist in you. Right at this moment within your pain body you may not experience your body as light, but the light and space are there. The essence is there, the nature is there, the energy is there. Everything is there. It's just a question of knowledge, attention, and habit, of your recognizing and entering the door.

What is the closest experience to the body of light you can have at this moment? To get a taste, think back to the first time you met a key person in your life, someone with whom you became very close. The instant of your meeting was pure—at first glance you may have seen only the vague form of a stranger in front of you. But in the moments that followed something interesting may have entered your awareness—the way the person tilted his head, the cut of his hair, the sound of his voice, or even the way he remained silent. You might have thought to yourself, "I love the silent type!" Some kind of familiarity lent itself to that first impression. Either you were drawn to a certain quality that you yourself lacked or you related to a quality that you both shared. From this first impression, you began to cultivate attachment. Over time, the more you related with the person and the more you got to know him, the stronger the attachment became. The bond grew stronger, denser, stickier, and grosser.

It is easy to understand how the three root poisons of ignorance, attachment, and aversion can evolve in any relationship. Over time, a relationship may become so gross, with so much anger or jealousy, that the only logical choice is to end it.

The point is, not just at the beginning of a relationship but at any beginning, the first moment of perception is pure and significant. There is a lightness and openness to it. From that moment either the root poisons will start to develop and your experience will grow heavy and unwieldy, or the sense of clear light will be maintained.

The history of the Tibetan Bön and Buddhist dzogchen traditions is rich with documented cases of great masters who have achieved the rainbow body, some as recently as the past century. For example, there are the biographies of the famous twenty-four Bön dzogchen masters of Zhang Zhung, each of whom taught the next of the masters in succession, and each of whom achieved the rainbow body. The body of light is the highest attainment of dzogchen practice. Unlike the teachings of sutra, dzogchen ("the Great Perfection") strongly emphasizes spontaneous perfection, awareness, and clarity. The teachings of tantra emphasize transformation, not self-liberation or spontaneous perfection. Neither sutra nor tantra has practices with the vision of light (*tögel* practices), which are unique to dzogchen and are the primary cause of achieving the body of light.

To most of us, disappearing into light at the time of death may seem an unreachable or unlikely goal. Yet, no matter how high these teachings are, gaining knowledge of how the body of light is attained has value for any meditation practitioner. The teachings of dzogchen not only present a potentially swift and direct path to enlightenment, they also give us an important understanding of the intimate relationship between body, energy, and mind—between channel, prana, and bindu, or *tsa*, *lung*, and *tiglé*—and point the way toward key signs of results from practice that are within reach.

WHAT IS THE BODY OF LIGHT?

According to the dzogchen teachings, your physical body is a product of your own impure vision. Your flesh, blood, bone, breath, heart, lungs, limbs, and sense organs are all manifestations in the physical dimension of the five natural elements. All the elements, in turn, arise directly from emotions that are caused by the lack of awareness of pure light and space. Your unique experience of the universe as a human being stems from this fundamental lack of self-awareness.

How can one purify the vision and attain the body of light? In brief, the process begins when an individual enters the spiritual path and seeks self-realization. Through connection with an authentic master and through dedicated study and practice, one develops recognition of and familiarity with the nature of mind. Increasingly, patterns of ignorance and dualistic vision are deconstructed within one's mind, one's energy, and one's body. The knot of the conceptual mind is gradually loosened and, at the point of final realization, the knot is untied. The physical dimension, which itself is a product of dualistic vision, is able to dissolve back into its source, into the base.

As one attains the body of light, any areas of the body that contain consciousness dissolve. The practitioner's body shrinks to a fraction of its original size or disappears completely and only the fingernails, toenails, and hair are left behind.

The basis of the body of light is recognition of the true self. Through this recognition, one's awareness becomes light and one's body becomes space. It is not called a "body of space," however, because light is more recognizable in our daily experience. This phenomenon is often referred to as the rainbow body, not just because of a rainbow's illusory nature, but also because rainbow displays often accompany a great master's dissolution into light. One might say that rainbows are the elements' way of responding to the beauty of the liberating spirit.

ONE ACCOUNT OF THE BODY OF LIGHT

Over the centuries there have been many recorded accounts of the external manifestations of the body of light. One recent example is the description below by Kelzang Tenpé Gyeltsen of the death of the famous Bönpo dzogchen master Shardza Tashi Gyeltsen Rinpoche, who attained the rainbow body in 1934 at age seventy-five. Shardza Rinpoche's teachings on the *Heart Drops of Dharmakaya* and his commentaries on dream yoga and Tibetan yoga (*trulkhor*), for example, continue to be studied and practiced widely in the Bön tradition today.

According to Kelzang Tenpé Gyeltsen, near the time of his passing, Shardza Rinpoche went to an uninhabited mountainside to meditate. After performing an elaborate feast offering, he sang songs of realization and then entered his small tent, sewed up the door, and ordered his disciples not to enter. He remained there continually in the five-point meditation posture.

> The next day, many great and small linked spheres of rainbow light and many kinds of horizontal and vertical lights shone above his tent. At night there were [many] rainbow lights, [including] an especially clear white light that was like a [white] woolen cloth appearing alone. After three days the ground shook and there was a loud noise and a gentle rain of flowers fell. After the fourth day variegated light emanated through the seams of the tent; the five different rainbow colors were vividly enveloping [each other] and arising like boiling misty vapor. Then, a genuine and holy disciple, Tsultrim Wangchuk—the best of all the practitioners—said, "If we leave [the master's] body for a long time now, there is the danger that there will be no remains at all as a support for our faith and our prayers in the future." Hurrying to meet [the master's] holy remains, he opened the door of the small tent and prostrated himself. He saw that the remains were envel-

oped in light and that they were elevated about one cubit in midair. He drew near to the presence [of his master]. Most of the nails of [the master's] hands and feet were strewn upon his seat. The body remained. It had transformed to about the size of a one-year-old child, and the heart was warm. Then the magnificent [disciple] Tsultrim Wangchuk dressed the precious body in the regalia of the Enjoyment Body.[5]

Many elements of Kelzang Tenpé Gyeltsen's description parallel other accounts of the body of light, with one notable exception: most students would not succumb to their attachment to their master's remains and enter the private space before the process is complete lest they disturb the final meditation and ultimate transformation.

THE NATURE OF SPACE, LIGHT, AND APPEARANCE

To understand the conditions that are necessary for the body to dissolve into pure space and light, you first need to understand the nature of this pure space and light and the pure appearances that arise from them. In the dzogchen teachings, space is commonly referred to as *the mother*, light as *the son*, and appearances as *energy*.

Space is called the mother because it is the source, the origin. All appearances arise from space, are hosted by space, and dissolve back into space. Space is known as *künzhi*, the base of all, the essence, the dharmakaya. The space referred to here is not the space within an empty room or the space an object takes up. It is our own nature, the empty nature of self. It is the space where we try to abide during meditation. It is the space from which we can observe our thoughts arising, the space into which they dissolve, the space of pure consciousness.

The mother is the base of both samsara and nirvana, the base of everything from the tiniest insect to the primordial Buddha Samantabhadra (Tib. Kuntuzangpo). It is omnipresent, pervasive, and changeless. There is nothing there you can point to. It is unobscured, rootless,

5. William M. Gorvine, trans., "The Pleasure Garden of Wish-Fulfilling Trees" (unpublished ms.).

naked, primordially undeluded. It cannot be improved or worsened by causes or conditions. It has no form, color, or shape. Space is like the sky—infinitely vast and boundless. It pervades everything, and everything is perfected in it.

Light is called the son because it arises from the mother and is inseparable from the mother. If the mother is the clear, empty sky, then the son is like the sun in the sky, the light that illuminates space. When we speak of this light, we are not referring to physical light or an appearance similar to a tree, a rock, or some other object appearing in space. Rather, we are referring to the subtle light of awareness, to the awareness of the base. When we abide in deep meditation and connect with the vast openness of space where subtle dualities are dissolved, recognition of that space is the son. At the same time, that recognition is no different from what is being recognized. It is self-realization. Mother and son are inseparable: there is no awareness without emptiness; there is no emptiness without awareness.

This luminous self-awareness of the mind is known as rigpa, the nature of mind, the clarity of the natural state, the sambhogakaya. The sense of clarity cannot be explained or analyzed by the conceptual mind. The son experiences just as a mirror experiences. Everything appears clearly there—color, beauty, form—but the mirror never analyzes, judges, or imputes. It is clear, direct perception in the base.

Appearances are referred to as *energy* because everything that appears in our experience is essentially composed of energy, everything from our random thoughts, recollections, and emotions to our sense perceptions. We may be thinking of our plans for today, remembering what we did yesterday, feeling angry in a traffic jam, or enjoying the taste of food—all appearance is energy. Energy is manifestation, the nirmanakaya. In the dzogchen tradition, energy in its purest aspect is referred to as *sound*, *light*, and *rays*. If rigpa is the sun of self-awareness that is lighting up all the sky, then sound, light, and rays are the sun's radiant energy that is illuminating all appearance.

Although we normally perceive external and internal appearances as having their own inherent existence, in absolute reality every object and person and the mind itself are empty. All appearances have the nature of space. In the first moment that sound, light, and rays arise, before our deluded mind can impute its dualistic perception, these three great visions are each experienced as a pure self-manifestation of our own primordial state, inseparable from the base.

▶ *Sound* is like an echo—sound that is returning to its source.

▶ *Light* is like a rainbow—the unconditioned aspect of luminosity that arises from emptiness, dwells in the empty nature of mind, and dissolves back into that empty nature.

▶ *Rays* are like the sun's rays—emanating out and reflecting back from all appearance.

How the Conditional Body Develops

If you recognize that every experience you have is nothing more than the pure energy of the inseparable state of space and light, experiences disturb you less. Energy and appearance are no longer an obstacle but instead are an unceasing opportunity to recognize your origin, your source. As long as you do not recognize your source and continue to see appearances as independent, separate entities, then you remain trapped in the cycle of samsara.

Your ability to recognize has particularly important ramifications at the time of death. That transition is called the Great Moment because your level of understanding and awareness at that time can either propel you to liberation or consign you to rebirth in samsara. Soon after the last breath and the final dissolution of the elements, the clear light of death arises. At this profound moment, the consciousness is no longer veiled by the obscurations of the physical body or of the disturbing emotions, and the innate awareness appears very clearly. You experience the mother and son, inseparable space and light.

If you are familiar with the natural state, this moment presents a great opportunity to recognize that space is light, that light is space, and that light and space are energy—there is no separation. This recognition of no separation appears as clear light. Clear light is not white, yellow, blue, red, or green. It is pure awareness. The moment you realize that light, you are liberated; and the moment you are liberated, you realize that light. This moment of realization is Samantabhadra, Buddha, enlightenment.

However, if you fail to recognize the clear light and the primordial movement of sound, light, and rays as your own self-manifestation, then you are deluded in all experience. You are driven by your karmic patterns, and the development of the samsaric body—your next rebirth in the cycle of suffering—begins.

A teaching from the *Zhang Zhung Nyen Gyü* called "The Mirror of the Luminous Mind" describes this developmental process in detail (see appendix 1).[6] All the five natural elements arise, all the gross emotions manifest, your entire physical body evolves, and you become subject to birth, old age, sickness, and death simply because of your lack of recognition of the true nature of space, light, and appearance. As mind and prana become ever grosser, the object of mind consciousness also becomes grosser. This principle is illustrated by the well-known story of the lion who looked down a well and saw his own fearful appearance reflected back at him from the still water below. The lion roared at the reflection, and the reflection roared back. The lion roared louder, and the reflection roared back louder. What happened next? The lion pounced at his adversary, jumping to his death.

When you experience the sound, light, and rays, you don't realize them as being a pure reflection of your own self. Your mind sees what is illusory as concrete and separate. Ignorance, attachment, and aversion all spring from there. As soon as your mind grasps, it obscures itself. It fails to experience awareness, and therefore the base is obscured. This fundamental obscuration is called innate ignorance.

How Is the Body of Light Achieved?

Meditation practice can begin to reverse the process that formed this conditional body. You can return to the place where you actually connect with that clear light in yourself, realize that light in yourself, and fully manifest it. Put more simply, understanding is your doorway to enlightenment. When you realize, you are liberated. When you don't

6. In all cases where the *Zhang Zhung Nyen Gyü* is listed as the primary source, information is drawn from Lokesh Chandra, *History and Doctrine of Bon-po Nispanna-Yoga: Original Tibetan Texts on the Transmission, Teaching, and Deities of the Rolzogs Chen Zhan Zhan School of the Bon-po's* (New Delhi: International Academy of Indian Culture, 1968).

realize, you are deluded. Everything is a creation of the mind. Your conditional body developed over time from subtle to gross. Its dissolution can take place over time from gross to subtle. The gross physical body can dissolve into space, and the awareness can dissolve into light.

The dzogchen teachings offer two primary forms of meditation that bring one to this understanding through direct experience. One is *trekchö*, a practice of space; the other is *tögel*, a practice of light. As with any dzogchen practice, it is important to receive direct instruction and transmission from an experienced, qualified master to ensure that trekchö and tögel are practiced correctly. After completing the foundation practices, serious dzogchen practitioners may devote a lifetime to mastering these two.

Trekchö practice involves abiding continuously in awareness of the space into which both the observer and observed have dissolved. The Tibetan term *trekchö* means "cutting through." One trekchö practice, for example, simply involves observing your thoughts, emotions, memories, or sensory experiences. If you feel angry, you can look inward to clearly and directly observe your feelings of anger, without analyzing or judging. This simple act of observation "cuts through" the anger, and the emotion immediately and spontaneously dissolves into space. Next, you observe the observer—the one who has been observing the anger—and the observer also dissolves. You connect with that empty space and you abide there in single contemplation as long as possible without elaboration.

Tögel practice is essentially trekchö practice plus work with vision. As with trekchö, you observe, dissolve, and abide; at the same time, you continuously maintain awareness of the movement of sound, light, rays, and other visions without being distracted by these appearances and losing the ground of awareness of space. Absolute stability in the nondual contemplation of trekchö is necessary for developing the visions and experiences of tögel practice. One tögel method is performed in the dark; another while gazing at the sky; another while gazing indirectly at the sun. In addition, maintaining specific tögel postures while meditating helps to open the channels and permit the flow of specific forms of energy (wind, prana), thus allowing specific experiences of the mind and supporting the experience of tögel visions. When done skillfully, these practices enable you to "see" the nature of mind projected externally as though it were in front of you, permitting you to become familiar with the self-nature of all vision.

Ultimately, tögel practice allows you to integrate your meditative experiences with all experiences. Normally, it is difficult to look around you at people or things and remain internally clear, yet no experience need interfere with self-awareness.

THE LIGHT IS ALWAYS THERE

I should reemphasize that, in these practices, the space and light are not something we are trying to generate or chase after. They are not "over there" somewhere or phenomena that can only exist in your future. The space and light are here, now. They exist in all areas of your experience and your being. We are all beings of light. Even as the form changes from subtle to gross and back again, the essence does not change. You need only learn to recognize the essence that is already there.

The physical body dissolving into the rainbow body is similar, in a way, to ice melting into water. Frozen water seems solid and substantial, yet it has the same nature as fluid water. As ice melts, you no longer make the distinction between ice and water. Similarly, as the impure elements and karmic traces dissolve into pure space and light, there is no more distinction between the gross physical body and the nature of mind.

There is a teaching called "The Six Lamps" that guides us in recognizing the clear light energy in all levels of our existence. Basically, we learn to recognize the light of self-awareness that exists:

- ▶ in the vast, infinite space that is the base of all
- ▶ in the space within our heart center
- ▶ in the subtle channels connecting the heart with the eyes
- ▶ in our own organs of perception
- ▶ in all external visions
- ▶ in the visions we experience in the bardo, the transitional state between death and rebirth.

The light in all six spaces has different qualities, yet in the end there is only one light and only one space, and this space and light are inseparable. Imagine that in a dark room there is a lamp fashioned from a doll. The doll is entirely hollow, its eyes formed by cutouts. A light bulb has been affixed within the doll's heart. When the bulb is lit, it illuminates itself as well as the space around it. Furthermore, the light rises up and out through the eye openings, thus illuminating any object placed in front of the eyes.

Imagine now that you are that doll. The same light that pervades all of space, all your experiences of life, is emanating as innate self-awareness from your heart. It is rising up through the channels to your eyes. Everything within your line of sight you see only because it is illuminated by and reflects this same light of self-awareness, the same light that arises from the core of your being.

The abiding light in the heart, the arising light in the channels, the appearing light outside the eyes, and the projected light on the surrounding objects—all the levels of experiencing light may be different in terms of location and characteristics but are not different in terms of quality and essence.

▶──────────────────────────────────────

The Six Lamps

According to the teaching of the Six Lamps from the *Zhang Zhung Nyen Gyü*, the natural energy of the primordial state can be seen as six lamps, or lights. The six lamps are recognized as follows:

1. **The light of künzhi, the mother, the base.** This first lamp is the clear light of emptiness, the unbounded pure presence that is like a fully illuminated sky. Like sunshine in a clear, open sky, this light pervades all that appears and exists; it universally pervades all of samsara and nirvana and is not limited by any confines. It is unmodified, uncontrived, and spontaneously perfect. This is known as *the lamp of the abiding base.*

2. **The light of self-arising innate awareness within the heart.** This light of rigpa is no different from the light of künzhi or any of the other lamps. It is all-pervasive like the sun in a vast, cloudless sky. But in this case, you sense its location in the center of the heart.

Your essence, your whole being is felt in the vast space within the depths of the heart. This light of awareness is called *the lamp of the physical heart.*

3. **The light of penetrating wisdom that moves through the channels.** There are two energy channels leading from the heart to the eyes. If you close your eyes and connect with the light in the heart, you can sense a spontaneous arising of rigpa as it flows unimpeded from the heart to the eyes. This light is known as *the lamp of the soft white channel.*

4. **The light of naked awareness before experience is divided into particular forms or entities.** As the third light arises from the heart and you open your eyes, you can see the light of innate awareness. Here, you are resting your gaze as though gazing at the sky without grasping at any objects that fall within your line of vision. You continue to feel the same deep space within the heart penetrating through the channels, through the eyes, and resting in the sky. This is called *the watery lamp of the far-reaching lasso.*[7]

5. **The light of naked nondual awareness that underlies the apparent division into subject and object.** This is the light of rigpa as it manifests as any object of your awareness. Now you allow your vision to rest on objects before you. When the mind is left in its own state and does not perceive or engage objects by means of cognition, the base of all brilliantly manifests without obscuration. The appearances of objects arise vividly clear like reflections in a mirror. Because you are not disconnected from the space and continue to perceive the same light that pervades the base, you experience the sacred in appearances. You realize the three kayas in appearances. You realize the light in appearances. This is known as *the lamp of pointing out the pure dimension.*[8]

6. **The light of samsara and nirvana.** At the time of death, if you have learned to recognize and familiarize yourself with this light that pervades all your experience, you will have less or no fear. Even with the loss of your physical body, you do not experience losing

---

7. It is also referred to as *the water lamp that lights the distance.*
8. It is also referred to as *the lamp of introduction to the pure land.*

your self. Because innate awareness has attained its own place, you do not chase after appearances and are freed from the illusion that self-arising appearances exist externally. Confusion is cleansed and purified. This light is the sixth lamp, *the lamp of the bardo.*

◀

THE BODY OF LIGHT IN DAILY LIFE

You can begin the process of the body of light before learning the dzogchen practices: you need only work with your own awareness, attitudes, and behavior. The initial results may not be measured in awesome rainbow displays but are experienced as increased feelings of openness, lightness, and other improvements in your day-to-day life.

The teachings tell us that the body of light is possible. If that is so—if you can actually dissolve concrete substance into space and light—then certainly it is possible to transform depression into light, for example. Every painful block, whether emotional, physical, or psychological, can be transformed, removed, minimized, or prevented.

The most loving relationship can stay loving, for example, if you can recognize and prevent any discord in its earliest stages. Failed relationships are often founded on simple feelings of self-doubt or insecurity. For example, imagine that one day you ask your partner to wash the dishes, and your partner leaves them unwashed. You notice those unwashed dishes, you think about those unwashed dishes, you focus on them, you obsess about them, and because of your self-doubt, for the first time you become very agitated. The other person has no other choice but to react in turn, and this leads to a big argument. If the negative interactions intensify and continue, you may start to develop negative feelings about your partner. In time you may start to feel that this person is the obstacle of your life, that you can't be with this person any longer, that the relationship can't go on. The problem is no longer about washing dishes, it's no longer about action, words, or attitudes, it's about the person: "*You* are the problem." But if you look back closely, you'll see that the story started in a moment that became tainted by discomfort and insecurity.

You must ask yourself: How well can you maintain and reinforce your purer qualities? How much of what you say or do at the beginning of a relationship comes from a place of awareness rather than from a sense of powerlessness driven by conditions?

This principle applies to nearly every area of life. If you feel your job is overwhelming, think back to the moment when you first received the job offer. If you feel your house is depressing to live in, think back to the moment when you first walked through its rooms. At first sight you may have glimpsed the divine, or at least the experience was neutral. There was no sense of grasping; there was just space. From that moment the conditional job or the conditional house began to take shape.

The sense of being overwhelmed or dissatisfied is all a matter of perception. Just as you can dissolve the conditional body back into the original space and light, you can dissolve your gross states of mind back to a place of greater openness and clarity. Imagine how it would feel to dispel the biggest confusion or conflict of your life. Suppose you finally reconciled with a close relative after years of not speaking or you finally retired from a stressful, boring job. How would you feel in your body, energy, and mind? That is a glimpse of the experience of the body of light. There is the presence of light in that space. At the close of a deep session of meditation or of a weeklong spiritual retreat, the natural experience of luminosity and lightness you feel is also part of the process of developing the body of light. All of your meditation practice is about trying to develop this emptiness and clarity. And in a way, doing so is to dissolve the gross physical elements.

However, we always tend to gravitate toward the grosser experiences. We tend to visit stressful places, watch stressful news reports, or do too much stressful work. We seek out the people who have caused us pain and suffering, and we confront them at the wrong time and in the wrong space without doing any advance preparation. In our minds, as well, we'll make time to visit disappointments and other painful experiences without being aware we're doing it. We'll make these visits while waiting for a bus, while taking a coffee break, or while lying in bed at night. If you pay attention to how often you visit these kinds of negative experiences, you may be surprised. It happens effortlessly, and it becomes a pattern.

If you bring awareness into your thoughts and actions, you can make more of your visits from a state of clarity, strength, and groundedness. Another option is to introduce more positive behaviors into your life. I recommend to people who are feeling depressed, for example, that they consistently take time each day to change their patterns of behavior:

► List five places in your house, neighborhood, or town where you feel comfortable, such as a porch, shrine room, neighborhood park, or garden. Visit one of these places on a daily basis and sit there. When you experience a positive quality of peace or calm or safety, bring this feeling inside so you connect with this as an internal quality.

► List five people with whom you have contact who make you feel uplifted or energized. Spend time with one of these people each day, or every other day. Have tea together, take a walk, or engage socially in a simple way.

► List five activities that bring you pleasure, such as walking, cooking, or listening to or making music. Engage in one of these activities each day.

If you consistently follow this advice, over time the positive qualities of joy and enthusiasm will become a natural part of who you are.

Short meditation practices on a regular basis are also helpful. The next time you feel overwhelmed and confused, find a serene, inspiring place to sit and meditate. Try looking inward at your situation from a perspective of clear, direct, open awareness, without judging or analyzing. Connect with feelings of spaciousness and groundedness. You may find that within just a few minutes all your feelings of being overwhelmed will dissolve into space and light.

It is one thing to change your entire body into light; it is another to change your identity as a pain body. You don't have to feel overburdened and overwhelmed. With just a few simple changes to your day, things can be lighter, clearer, and more spacious.

Practices of the Body 4

THE SIMPLE DZOGCHEN meditation practice of direct, open, non-analytical observation is a way to turn any experience of body, speech, or mind into a doorway to enlightenment. The Bön Buddhist teachings offer other practices and postures that particularly emphasize the body as a doorway. Detailed instructions for several of them appear in the pages to come.

Certain methods promote a sense of stillness in the body. Some work with the movements of prana in the body, others incorporate physical movement and release. Each of these plays a key role in meditation practice; for this reason, many practitioners combine a variety of different practices in their daily routine for a more complete experience.

ABIDING IN THE FIVE-POINT MEDITATION POSTURE

Many meditation practitioners don't realize how the way they sit influences the quality of their meditation, but the effects are real: if you hold your body in a particular position, immediately that position will provide some experiences that were not there before.

The five-point meditation posture described below helps to open and guide the flow of energy, or prana, through your body. According to dzogchen, this has the effect of lessening distracting thoughts and releasing other obstacles to meditation so that you can more easily connect with and abide in the nature of mind. The teachings of tantra say that this posture "conquers and imprisons" the conceptual thoughts.

Body, prana, and mind are brought together as one in a posture of clear, open awareness.

When the energy flow is not open and guided, you have the opposite experience: Your mind seems to hop around like a monkey in every direction. You don't know which direction your next thought will come from or where it will take you. Or your mind becomes dull. For example, we may see a businessman walking to work in the morning, standing tall with an open chest, but by eight in the evening, we may see him slumped in his subway seat. The morning posture evokes fire-like energy and clarity to help him greet the business day; the evening posture evokes dullness and sleepiness, with the effect of closing down his tired, stressed mind.

Army recruits are required to adopt a very erect, open posture because that position inspires the power, confidence, and readiness that are essential to the battlefield. The hunched posture of that old man I used to walk past in Italy, seated on his park bench, was telling a lot of stories about his past. I could see in his shoulders and neck all about his life in the war, his family-related losses, and the exhaustion of his life and business. Yet in a single moment he could have thought to himself, "I know I'm feeling this way, but I'm going to change the position of my body as best I can." He could have sat up, expanded his chest, and straightened his neck and spine. With these changes the man would have immediately felt an internal shift away from his pain body—and would have felt a bit less distracted and more uplifted, connected, balanced and centered, with a more open flow of energy.

When the mind is contracted, it is difficult to open it through mind alone. It is easier to change the way you breathe than it is to change your mind; and it is easier to change your physical posture than it is to change your breath. You can learn to change what is easiest to change in whatever way will support your meditation practice.

In the Tibetan Bön Buddhist tradition, the five points of the five-point meditation posture are as follows:[9]

9. To learn more about the channels and chakras of the energy body, see chapter 12, "Mind and Prana in Meditation Practice."

Figure 4.1. Five-point meditation posture
(see also plate 1)

1. Sit cross-legged. This helps to prevent the pranic energy from being dispersed, and it generates internal heat, supporting the deeper, subtler, more blissful experiences of meditation practice.
2. Fold your hands in the position of equipoise. Rest your hands palm up, left hand on right, against the lower part of your belly about four finger-widths below the navel. The Tibetan term for this posture point is *nyamzhag*, where *nyam* means "equal" and *zhag* means "abide." What is made equal? Clarity and emptiness. This hand position maximizes your ability to abide in the balanced state of inseparable clarity and emptiness, and it minimizes the experience of duality—the judgmental activity of the mind and the sense of separation or disconnectedness.
3. Keep your spine straight. Holding your spine erect but relaxed keeps the primary channels straight and open to allow smooth and easy upward flow of prana.
4. Tuck your jaw slightly down and in. This lengthens the back of your neck and helps to quiet your thoughts.
5. Keep your chest open. This aids free breathing and helps to open your heart chakra, a central energetic focal point of the body.

THE WHITE LIQUID PRACTICE TO HEAL DISEASE

In ancient times yogis and practitioners used methods of energetic and pranic healing to overcome obstacles to meditation and improve their health. This is one such practice from "The Pith Instruction of Tsa Lung (Channels and Winds)," a chapter from the *Zhang Zhung Nyen Gyü*.

Healing of the body is more complete when it occurs on many levels. Consider that any time you have a disease or injury, you suffer from more than just the negative physical sensations. You may also carry around within you some kind of mental image or mental or energetic block associated with the pain, discomfort, fear, or events surrounding the illness or injury. This image or block is as much a part of your sense of your body as the actual pain or discomfort is. It can linger in you for days, months, or even years.

For example, after a traumatic experience with cancer, some people may live the rest of their lives identifying with an image of diseased tissue or of chemotherapy treatments even if their cancer was completely eradicated. Harboring mental images such as these can slow your recovery, limit the freedom to enjoy life, and be an obstacle to the open awareness of meditation.

I recommend the White Liquid Practice to Heal Disease for any physical illness or injury. The practice can have profound physical benefits as it opens the chakras (energetic centers of your body) and purifies obscurations and obstacles to your practice. If you do the practice consistently and correctly, in time your mental images of any disease or injury will become associated more with bliss and spaciousness than with pain, discomfort, or mental or energetic blocks.

This practice is best done with guidance from an experienced, knowledgeable master. To do it effectively, you must maintain the correct position of the body as described below, visualize the five seed syllables in their correct positions,[10] and follow the directions for breathing and visualization.

The practice is done in the following way:

Connect with higher wisdom (through the practice of guru yoga).

---

10. Seed syllables are sacred characters from the Tibetan alphabet that represent, in a pure way, our connection with our highest nature. For more information about seed syllables, see part 2, "Ceaseless Speech."

Pray to the enlightened beings, asking them to "Please purify me and bless me so I may have success in this healing practice."

Squat on the floor with arms crossed, hands on knees, spine as straight as possible, head tilted slightly down, and the big toe of your left foot pressing on the big toe of your right foot (see figure 4.2). This position creates the physical pressure necessary for generating heat and promoting upward-moving energy. If the position is too uncomfortable, you can add support, while still maintaining pressure, by placing a cushion under your heels or buttocks.

Now, imagine an energetic channel running through the center of your body from the area of the sexual organs through your heart to above the crown of your head. Imagine that in this central channel and on the soles of the feet there are five seed syllables, as shown in figure 4.3. Visualize a seed syllable at each of five locations:

- A green *YAM* on the sole of each foot, representing the air element
- A red *RAM* at the secret chakra in the area of the sexual organs, representing the fire element
- A red *OM* at the heart chakra
- A white *A* at the throat chakra
- A white, upside-down *HAM* above the top of the crown.

Figure 4.2. Meditation posture for the White Liquid
Practice to Heal Disease

Each syllable faces out, as shown in the illustration. If you cannot maintain a mental image of a syllable at least try to visualize its color and feel the quality it represents.

As you maintain the posture and visualize the seed syllables, breathe in deeply and exhale the stale breath. Repeat three times. Then, to activate the prana, take in a deep breath of pure air, inhaling it into the secret chakra, and hold. Normally air is experienced as entering the lungs, but for this practice imagine and feel that the air is being inhaled

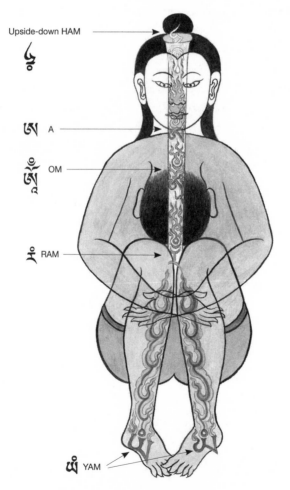

Figure 4.3. Visualization for the White Liquid Practice
to Heal Disease (see also plate 6)

deeply into the secret chakra. While holding, feel that the breath and your diaphragm are pressing downward, and at the same time contract lightly upward with the muscles of the perineum and anus so that the upward pressure meets the downward pressure. Hold the breath in this way for as long as you can.

While continuing to hold the breath, visualize generating healing flames: Clearly see and feel the air quality of the green *YAM* at the soles of the feet. Imagine and feel that the upward pressure from contracting the muscles at the base of the pelvis causes the air energy to move gradually upward. As soon as the air touches the red fire of *RAM* in the secret chakra, the fire blazes. The flames move straight up through the central channel where they first touch the red *OM* in the heart and then the white *A* in the throat. Like rocket boosters, the *OM* and the *A* each additionally fuel the flames.

The blazing hot fire moves up through the brain and into the crown chakra. As soon as it touches the white, upside-down *HAM*, the *HAM* melts into a divine liquid—a blissful, creamy white nectar that drops down through all the nerves and channels of the body, especially into areas where there is pain or disease. See and feel the warm nectar flow into diseased lungs, torn ligaments, injured disks or inflamed skin, any areas where you experience pain, numbness, or general malaise.

With the nectar's flow, feel the removal of disease and pain. This liquid of the melted *HAM* is felt both as a warm physical sensation and as a deep quality of bliss. Sense the bliss on three levels:

▸ *on the mind level* as a flow of subtle consciousness
▸ *on the pranic level* as a flow of healing energy
▸ *on the physical level* as a flow of creamy nectar

Visualize and feel the blissful nectar dropping down not only into areas of your physical body but also into any mental images you associate with pain, injury, or disease. For example, allow the nectar to flow into the image of receiving chemotherapy for lung cancer, the image of a car accident where whiplash occurred, the image of teeming microbes, or the image of a caustic, dark cloud where a breast used to be.

When the healing nectar enters each of the physical areas and images, see and feel it merging with them and transforming them completely, clearing away all disease, pain, and injury and creating clear space in their place. More and more, feel the opening of that space that is the absence of disease and pain and feel the increasing presence of light and bliss within the space.

Abide in the experience. When it diminishes, repeat the practice.

When you finish the practice, dedicate its merit to the benefit of all sentient beings.

TIBETAN YOGA: SIX VIGOROUS PHYSICAL MOVEMENTS THAT OVERCOME NEGATIVE EMOTIONS

Physical exercise can be good for the body, good for the energy, good for the mind, and good for the spirit. Think of how you feel when you've been inactive for a long time and you start jogging or taking brisk walks. Before you might have been feeling moody, stressed out, and foggy-minded, but after exercising you feel better physically, with a freer flow of energy, a clearer mind, and a more uplifted spirit.

The vigorous "magical movements" of trulkhor (Tibetan yoga) exercise the body and have similar results. However, trulkhor was designed explicitly for its more targeted, subtle effects on the energy and mind. Specifically, the trulkhor exercises are an aid to meditation practice, a gateway to a more open, clear, and stable experience of abiding in the natural state of mind. By integrating vigorous physical movement with mental concentration and awareness of the breath, they unblock and open the flow of prana within specific areas of the body.

The six root trulkhor exercises described below have another unique effect: as they open and clear obscurations from certain areas of your physical body, they also help to free you from your negative emotions. By practicing them regularly, you can become less driven by anger, for example, and thus can be spontaneously more loving and abide with more stability in the natural state of mind. This ability to reduce your disturbing emotions through the door of the physical body is important to understand.

These six movements were designed by a master named Pöngyal Tsenpo and are from just one of four cycles in the "Quintessential

Instructions of the Oral Wisdom of the Magical Movements" from the *Zhang Zhung Nyen Gyü*. Some of the information here has also been drawn from a commentary to the text, "Oral Transmission [of Zhang Zhung] Magical Movements with Channels and Vital Breaths in the Great Treasury of Ultra Profound Sky," by the famous meditation master and scholar Shardza Tashi Gyeltsen Rinpoche (1859–1935), whose attainment of the rainbow body was described in chapter 3.

I strongly recommend that these exercises be done only with guidance from an experienced, qualified instructor to ensure that the mind has the right focus and to avoid the risk of injury through incorrect method. Unlike hatha yoga, the trulkhor postures involve continuous and often vigorous movement. If you have an injury or other limitation, ask your instructor to suggest modifications to the postures. People with health risks should consult a medical care provider before doing any vigorous exercises or movements that stress the joints.

How to Approach the Practice

With each trulkhor exercise, the practitioner:

1. assumes a specific posture as described below
2. inhales and holds the breath in a relaxed and pervasive manner, without tension or contraction
3. does seven repetitions of a physical movement while continuing to hold the breath
4. stands and shakes out the arms and legs, while exhaling forcefully through the nose, releasing the stale breath, and sounding *HA… PHET! ("PEH!")*

It is through this combination of posture, focused holding of the breath, physical movement, and forceful exhalation that each trulkhor exercise loosens up and releases the physical, energetic, emotional, and mental blockages in specific areas of the body. The process can be likened to clearing a flexible pipe that's clogged with ice: No matter how hard you blow into the pipe you will not be able to remove the solid blockage, but if you first bend and twist the pipe, the ice will break up into small particles that you can then expel by blowing forcefully. The different trulkhor exercises have a similar effect in loosening blockages so they can be fully released with the breath.

While doing the movements, you should draw attention to the areas of the body that are physically engaged as well as to the particular negative emotion associated with those areas (see individual instructions below). While exhaling, try to feel the emotion being released with the breath and dissolving into space. At the same time, feel the physical and energetic opening in the areas that were engaged. As you rest in that sense of opening and release, let it lead you to a greater sense of openness that is felt in the core of your being. Within that greater openness you have a greater possibility to experience positive qualities such as love, wisdom, peacefulness, or generosity, and you can connect with the deeper aspects of your mind, your consciousness, and your being.

When doing the physical movements, try to extend the reach of each movement as far as you comfortably can without forcing. For example, when the instructions say to "try to touch your elbows to your knees," move the elbows as close to the knees as you comfortably can. If it is difficult to hold the breath throughout all seven repetitions, you can do fewer repetitions and try over time to work up to seven.

During the exhalation, with the sound *HA* you imagine and feel the release of disease, pain, emotions, energetic disturbances, and mental obscurations. Through sounding *PHET!* you imagine and feel that you are cutting the root of these obstacles and obscurations so they cannot return.

Instructions for the Six Movements

Specific instructions for each of the six movements are as follows:

1. The Athlete's Hammer That Strikes Anger

Kneel on the floor, knees separated at a distance of about a shoulder-width, ankles crossed. Feel your weight at the knees.

While holding the spine straight, clasp your hands behind your neck and tilt your head slightly back. Hold your elbows out to your sides,

Figure 4.4 The Athlete's Hammer That Strikes Anger

chest expanded, and maintain a slightly upward and unfocused, resting gaze.

Inhale and hold the breath. Continue holding the breath comfortably throughout the repetitions.

Bend your torso forward while bringing your elbows inward. Try to touch your elbows to your knees or bring them as close to the knees as possible. Return to the initial position (spine straight, elbows to sides).

Repeat seven times.

Stand erect; jump and shake out your arms and legs; then exhale forcefully through the nose and mouth, sounding *HA PHET!* at the exhalation's end. Maintain a slightly upward, unfocused, resting gaze.

Benefit: This movement removes anger and is associated with the space element. With this opening you have more possibility to experience the spontaneous arising of love. At the start of the exercise, connect with the feeling of openness; as you curl down, experience a closing down. With the exhalation, sense the release of anger and an opening in the area of the chest and heart. Connect with the pure space element. Rest in the unbounded experience of openness and love.

2. The Window of Wisdom That Overcomes Ignorance

Sit cross-legged, hands on hips, with thumbs clasping the hipbones and fingers resting on the abdomen, with your elbows to your sides. Bend forward and bring elbows to knees.

Inhale and hold the breath. Continue holding the breath comfortably throughout the repetitions.

Bend forward, trying to bring your forehead to the floor. Then roll backward until your neck touches the ground behind you. As you roll, keep elbows to knees to the best of your ability and maintain the cross-legged position. If your elbows slip off your knees, reestablish them as you come forward.

Repeat this forward/backward roll seven times.

Stand erect; jump and shake out your arms and legs; then exhale forcefully through the nose and mouth, sounding *HA PHET!* at the exhalation's end. Maintain a slightly upward, unfocused, resting gaze.

Note: The space formed in the tight triangle between body and elbow is known as the window of wisdom, an opening to your deeper nature.

Figure 4.5 The Window of Wisdom That
Overcomes Ignorance

Benefit: This movement removes ignorance and is associated with the earth element; with the removal of ignorance wisdom has more opportunity to spontaneously arise. At the end of the repetitions, try to allow any feelings of doubt to release with the breath. Sense the opening and connect with the strength, stability, and grounded quality of the earth element. Rest in the state beyond doubt.

3. *Spinning the Four Limbs Like a Wheel to Overcome Pride*

Sit cross-legged, each hand grasping the toes of the opposite foot (here your arms are not crossed).

Figure 4.6 Spinning the Four Limbs Like a Wheel to Overcome Pride

Inhale and hold the breath. While doing the movements continually hold the breath and maintain the cross-legged position and finger grip.

Roll backward until your neck meets the ground. (Your knees do not have to touch the floor behind you.) Then roll forward, rising up on your knees while straightening the body from the waist up.

Repeat this forward/backward roll seven times.

Stand erect; jump and shake out your arms and legs; then exhale forcefully through the nose and mouth, sounding *HA PHET!* at the exhalation's end. Maintain a slightly upward, unfocused, resting gaze.

Note: Expanding your chest upward during the forward roll will give more momentum for rising high on the knees. Use particular care not to force this exercise in order to avoid neck injury.

Benefit: This movement removes pride and is associated with the air element. As pride diminishes, you have more possibility to experience a sense of peacefulness. With the out-breath feel the release of pride and sense the opening in the areas engaged by the movement. Rest in the experience for a minute or two, connecting with the experience of spaciousness and openness. Feel peaceful within that space and sense the flexible, communicative qualities of the air element.

4. *Loosening the Knot to Overcome Desire*

Sit cross-legged. Place your thumbs in the same-side armpits, fingers pointing toward the heart, elbows fully extended to the sides, chest open, spine straight.

Inhale and hold the breath. Continue holding the breath comfortably throughout the movement.

Try to touch the right elbow to the left knee by twisting the body, then try to touch the left elbow to the right knee (or come as close as possible).

Repeat seven times.

Stand erect; jump and shake out your arms and legs; then exhale forcefully through the nose and mouth, sounding *HA PHET!* at the exhalation's end. Maintain a slightly upward, unfocused, resting gaze.

Note: Keep the chest open while twisting. Feel the stretch of muscles in the abdomen and upper back and on the sides of the body.

Figure 4.7 Loosening the Knot to Overcome Desire (see also plates 2 and 3)

Benefit: This movement removes attachment and desire and is associated with the fire element. As attachment decreases, there is more opportunity for generosity to spontaneously arise. With the out-breath allow any feelings of attachment to release. Sense the opening. Feel the creative, joyful energy of the fire element. Abide in the experience of open generosity.

5. Fluttering the Silk Tassel Skyward to Overcome Jealousy

Support the body on the left palm and the sole of the left foot. (If you cannot maintain balance during the movements, try supporting yourself with the side of the foot instead of the sole.)

Figure 4.8 Fluttering the Silk Tassel Skyward to Overcome Jealousy (see also plate 4)

Inhale and hold the breath. Continue holding comfortably throughout the repetitions.

Extend both the right leg and right arm, waving them gently skyward seven times like a flag fluttering in a light wind. Now support the body on the right palm and the sole of the right foot and wave seven times.

Stand erect; jump and shake out your arms and legs; then exhale forcefully through the nose and mouth, sounding *HA PHET!* at the exhalation's end. Maintain a slightly upward, unfocused, resting gaze.

Benefit: This movement removes jealousy and is associated with the water element. As jealousy dwindles, openness has more possibility to spontaneously arise. At the end of the repetitions, allow any feelings of jealousy to release with the breath. Sense a great opening and connect with the deep comfort, ease, and fluidity of the pure water element. Rest in this experience of openness, comfort, and fluidity.

6. The Tigress's Leap That Overcomes Drowsiness and Agitation

Stand with your feet a shoulder's width apart.

Inhale and hold the breath comfortably throughout the movements.

Bend down so your head is between your knees. Bring both your arms around behind the knees and back between the legs, and bring

Figure 4.9 The Tigress's Leap That Overcomes Drowsiness and Agitation

your fingers toward your ears, touching or lightly holding them if possible.

While maintaining this posture hop forward seven times, then backward seven times.

Stand erect; jump and shake out your arms and legs; then exhale forcefully through the nose and mouth, sounding *HA PHET!* at the exhalation's end. Maintain a slightly upward, unfocused, resting gaze.

Benefit: This movement removes drowsiness, dullness, and agitation as obstacles to meditation. As you exhale, try to feel the release of any dullness or agitation. Rest a few minutes in the experience of open equanimity that balances clarity and emptiness.

If you are interested in information of more depth, the "Quintessential Instructions" and its accompanying commentary offer greater detail about the benefits of the six "magical movements." Appendix 2 gives a summary of these benefits.

PROSTRATIONS: A PHYSICAL MOVEMENT THAT TAMES THE EGO AND PURIFIES

Doing prostrations brings body and mind together in a way that purifies and prepares you for spiritual practice. The Tibetan term for prostration is *chak tsel lo*, which means "beneficial cleansing and purification."

When I lived in the monastery as a youngster, we always did prostrations at the beginning of classes. Typically, you will do three prostrations before receiving teachings, before sitting in meditation, or when reencountering a lama after a long absence.

The prostration is an integral part of the spiritual traditions of Tibet as well as of many other cultures. Although some Tibetan masters don't teach prostrations to their Western students, I feel that doing them is important in dharma practice. All of our intentions for entering into spiritual development inevitably have to do with our wish to tame the ego; it is only by minimizing and eventually completely overcoming the ego that we can achieve liberation. Doing prostrations is a helpful way to cultivate humility and minimize aggressiveness and arrogance.

There is no way to perform the physical act of bowing or prostrating without doing so from a place of respect, humbleness, and minimum ego. Prostration itself is inseparable from these qualities. If you are able to prostrate, you will have those qualities. If you are unable to prostrate—if the movement feels too inappropriate, out of character, or simply wrong—then clearly you are unable to connect with a real sense of respect and humility.

Doing prostrations also symbolizes our entering an important stage in the spiritual process. I remember when a certain student of mine arrived at that stage. He was a person who always did what he wanted in life from a place of stubbornness and very strong ego. Eventually, through receiving the teachings and doing the practice, he became tired of his mind-set. One day he came to me and said, "I'm trying to work on this part of myself. I will listen to someone now. I will be humble and follow someone. I will minimize my doubts and egoistic discussions and exercise my openness, trust, and respect." Prostrations express this same attitude and intent. They have the same sense of offering and the same sincere request for assistance in purifying the ego and closing the doors to the negative emotions.

Other Benefits

Doing prostrations has additional benefits: it trains the mind, generates devotion, cultivates a sense of refuge, accumulates merit, and purifies the negative karma of body, speech, and mind. For this reason many people do prostrations at least three times a day as part of their regular practice. There are people who are committed to doing one hundred or more daily prostrations, and serious students of the foundational practices of *ngöndro* try to accumulate one hundred thousand prostrations over a period of months or years.

Prostrations also benefit the body. Tibetan medicine does not separate physical and emotional health from spiritual health, and some physical or emotional problems may be seen as a manifestation of a deep accumulation of negative karma, particularly illnesses or infections that persist or recur over long periods of time. Tibetan medical doctors commonly prescribe prostrations because they burn away the negative energies and karma that contribute to illness and negative thoughts.

To Whom We Prostrate

In Buddhism, when we prostrate, we do so to the Three Jewels: the Buddha, the Dharma, and the Sangha. In the Tibetan spiritual traditions, we sometimes refer to a fourth jewel, the Lama.

The Lama is the master, the one who teaches and transmits to us the words of the Buddha.

The Buddha refers to the historical Buddha and to all other beings, male or female, who have achieved full enlightenment. Ultimately, when prostrating to the Buddha, we are prostrating to the state of enlightenment itself.

The Dharma is the knowledge that is our means for attaining liberation, the knowledge we access through the sacred texts and the words of the teacher. We value this knowledge and the texts so highly because without them there would be no way for us to achieve enlightenment.

The Sangha refers to the bodhisattvas—those who have achieved *bodhichitta*, those whose compassion has ripened, who are devoted to attaining liberation for the benefit of all sentient beings.[11]

Always visualize the jewels as higher than yourself—in front of and above you—just as your own shrine at home should always be higher than you when you are sitting, and just as when meeting with the lama you should always try to sit in a lower position as a gesture of respect.

How to Prostrate

There are two forms of prostration, one short and one long. The long form involves stretching out flat on the ground and is not described here. This is how the short prostration is performed in the Bön tradition:

Maintaining a continuous, flowing movement throughout the entire prostration, raise your arms up high in front of you, palms up. As you do so, visualize and feel that you are offering up to the master or to

---

11. In more casual usage *sangha* can refer to the community of monastics, or commonly in the West, to the broader community of meditation practitioners.

Figure 4.10 The Prostration
(see also plate 11)

the three or four jewels all the purity and beauty in the universe, everything you love and care about, even the things, ideas, and experiences to which you feel very attached. You may offer up beautiful flowers, favorite foods, the objects you love. Offering cultivates merit and is also a way to cultivate detachment.

Release the offering. As you start to bring the hands down, at about forehead level close the hands in a prayerful gesture and touch them to your forehead (to receive empowerment of the body), to your throat (to receive empowerment of the speech), and to your heart (to receive empowerment of the mind). Visualize and feel that you receive these empowerments from the enlightened beings in the form of light.

Sweep the palms downward from the waist across your thighs as you visualize sweeping away all the negative karma of body, speech, and mind.

Maintaining the smooth flow of movement, go down on hands and knees and touch your forehead to the floor. The moment all five points touch the floor—forehead, both hands, both knees—the doors are sealed to the five negative emotions of ignorance, attachment, hatred, jealousy, and pride.

Stand up, and with hands in the gesture of prayer, touch them to your heart. See the environment around you as reflecting more peaceful, pure, and enlightened qualities and see those same positive qualities in the people around you.

PART 2

Ceaseless Speech
gagpa mépé sung

Introduction to Speech 5

From the inseparable state of light and space,
the infinite compassion of the seed syllables naturally arises.
—"THE BIRTHLESS SPHERE OF LIGHT,"
A CHAPTER OF THE *MA GYÜ* (BÖN *MOTHER TANTRA*)

ONCE WHEN I was a young monk in India, after I went to bed one night, I started to hear a sound of constant banging. My bedroom was upstairs in the monastery, a large, glass-walled room used for cultivating mushrooms. The banging sound echoed loudly off the glass walls, and I soon became convinced someone was breaking my door down. It was only after I screamed out my window and brought all the lamas and monks running that I learned it was the sound of someone chopping wood down by the river—everyone joked that my screams had been much louder than the banging sound.

That is how it happens: every sound you hear is pure sound, but somehow it translates immediately into something else. You perceive it as a threat, or sometimes it calls you, invites you. Your conceptual mind translates it into whatever subtle or gross emotional state you are in, and you are drawn into the experience of pain speech. It is only by removing any filters and disengaging your conceptual mind that you can connect in a purer way to sound's energy.

Sound originates from space and is transmitted through space with the help of form. When sound is associated with conceptual thought or disturbing emotions, it leads you to ignorance and pain. When sound is more directly related to its original source, to emptiness, it is a doorway to the divine. At its purest, sound is one with space.

As we shift our focus from the body to speech, an entirely new set of doorways to enlightenment is revealed in the form of the sound-related practices of the Tibetan spiritual traditions. Speech as a doorway refers not just to speech per se, but to all forms of sound. In its purest aspect, speech refers to energy and vibration, or prana. Prana is much more than a mystical healing energy associated with Eastern disciplines such as acupuncture, t'ai chi or yoga; it is the fundamental energy of the basis of all existence, the energy from which every experience arises.

A patchwork of ancient knowledge about sound can be found throughout the Bön teachings: in tantra, in dzogchen, and even in Tibetan medicine. This part of the book brings the core elements of these sound practices together in a unified manner to enable a deeper understanding of technique in sound practice and to permit you to explore the practices that may make the most sense for you personally. There are instructions here for everything from chanting a seed syllable to cure a headache to using inner sound to connect deeply with the clear and blissful experience of the nature of mind.

If the body is initially thought of as the doorway of physical manifestation, then speech and sound are the doorway of the energetic dimension. Sound vibration, when synchronized with mind, has the capacity to heal all aspects of body, energy, and mind. The healing that sound offers can become the basis of your happiness and vitality. It can enrich your life, filling you with energy and light. These qualities, in turn, can enrich your spiritual development.

HEARING PURE SOUND

Speech at its highest is *ceaseless speech*. To understand the meaning of *ceaseless*, consider the opposite experience: the nagging sense that our possessions, relationships, or other important aspects of life will be depleted or come to an end or that they have never been complete even from the beginning. It is normal for us to go about our lives continually feeling that we are missing something, that we need *more* to be complete.

Ceaseless refers to the truth that all the qualities that you most want and need in order to feel complete and fulfilled are ever present and ever arising. Love, compassion, joy, equanimity, all the immeasurable wisdom qualities have always been here in you, unceasingly, in their perfected state. When you can connect deeply with this truth, there is infinite potential for the qualities to manifest whenever your external circumstances call for them. When we speak of *ceaseless*, therefore, it means that when your circumstances call for joy, joy comes. If love, compassion, or equanimity is called for, the quality spontaneously arises. The qualities, the energy, never ends. This is the sambhogakaya, the complete, perfected, and unceasing aspect of the natural state of mind.

In the West we often talk of the mind-body connection or of mind, body, and spirit, and speech is seldom mentioned. Yet, when you can listen to the experience of silence that is at the base of all speech, you can open to the potentiality, the light, the awareness of the natural state of mind. When you continuously abide there and just listen to the silence—the inner silence, the outer silence, like a calm, quiet lake without ripples—it is so beautiful. There is life and liveliness in this silence, and by being aware of it, it gives us what we lack. This is the silence from which all enlightened speech manifests. All speech that is clear and warm manifests from here.

Of course, we don't all experience this unceasing aspect through the sounds we hear. Whether you perceive sound as being painful and provocative or unceasing and perfected has everything to do with your state of mind. If you listen to a sound with fear, you will hear a threat. If you listen through clear, open awareness, you will instead experience its pure, clear nature.

CONNECTING WITH THE SOURCE

How did pure sound originate? The higher tantric explanation appears in the quotation that begins this chapter. According to the Bön *Mother Tantra*, when one realizes the inseparable state of light and space, or of clarity and emptiness, what spontaneously arises from that state is a seed syllable, such as one of the five warrior seed syllables, *A, OM,*

HUNG, RAM, and *DZA.* This subtle seed of wisdom manifests either as energy or as physical sound.

Just as the seed syllable has its origin in pure space and light and is inherently pure, giving voice to a seed syllable is a way to connect back to the source. A seed syllable is neither an actual character from the Tibetan alphabet, nor is it even the gross sound that you hear as the syllable is chanted in meditation practice. It is a subtle, inaudible vibration that is experienced in relation to mind. However, the visual appearance of a Tibetan letter and the sound and vibration of the voice do represent this subtle vibration. Focusing on image or sound helps to bring your mind in sync with the subtle vibration and with the deep, pure quality associated with it. When the syllable is synchronized with mind, it affects mind.

The entire Tibetan alphabet is composed of sacred syllables, and for this reason Tibetans treat the alphabet with great respect. Many of them avoid throwing their correspondence and other printed material in the trash and instead burn them, using the pure element of fire to dissolve their contents. They will not place a newspaper on the ground or step over a book. For some Western students, however, even the idea of chanting a Tibetan seed syllable in meditation practice may seem foreign or silly. Yet the use of *OM* and other seed syllables has its roots in ancient teachings by enlightened individuals who awakened through these sounds, realized their power, and saw how they could be used by others as a true doorway to enlightenment.

When various syllables of the Tibetan alphabet are sounded as mantra, they have the power to heal our physical, energetic, and mental disturbances. They help us to visualize transforming into enlightened tantric deities, connect with elemental qualities, or enter the state of rigpa. Reciting a mantra that comprises all the vowels and consonants of the alphabet is a way to purify pain speech. When sounded alone, different syllables can affect specific organs and chakras of the body.

Some students relate very quickly to the power of sound to help them arrive at a deeper connection in meditation practice. Not everyone can just sit with an unfocused gaze, let go of their thoughts, and rest unsupported with stable, open awareness in the nature of mind. People are so used to actively engaging—to touching, viewing, listening, or analyzing. Even the most experienced practitioners occasionally need support in focusing their awareness when they are subjected to meditative disturbances such as agitation or dullness.

Some people find more stability with visual support, such as focusing on the external image of the Tibetan letter *A*. Others do well with sound. Sound is a particularly intimate support for meditation practice since it is so closely related with your breath (prana), your mind, and your self.

Both sound and image engage the conceptual mind as they support awareness. Therefore, the higher levels of thought-free contemplation in dzogchen meditation are more easily achieved by practicing with self-arising sound—sound that arises spontaneously from your own nature, as described below. Through connecting with self-arising sound, you are able to experience the nature of mind in its nakedness.

PURITY THROUGH VIRTUE

Every sound is self-arising and is a doorway to enlightenment. Every sound is fundamentally pure. Yet not all speech and sound is experienced in a pure way. As we saw before, the sound of chopping wood can be translated as a madman breaking down a door. The most innocent comment by a stranger can ignite strong anger. It is only when speech is connected with awareness that it becomes aware speech. Awareness has everything to do with the purity of sound. This principle is the key to using sound as a doorway.

▸ **Abandoning the nonvirtues.** Certain forms of speech definitely support higher levels of awareness and therefore have higher perceived levels of purity. For example, it is easier to maintain open awareness when reassuring someone with gentle, loving words than when saying something spiteful. So, a basic way to begin purifying your speech is to become conscious of the effects of your choice of language. Using the approach of sutra, you can choose virtuous or neutral speech over nonvirtuous speech.

Sutra describes four types of virtuous speech, each of which involves refraining from engaging in one of the forms of nonvirtuous speech.[12] These four virtues are:

▷ *Abandoning the act of telling lies.* If you can be more precise and truthful in how you communicate, your speech will be more clear, direct, and infused with awareness as a result. This doesn't necessarily mean you should refrain only from telling outright lies. It also means speaking in ways that correspond more closely to your feelings and your beliefs. If you say "I like that," when you don't really like it, or "I'll try to stop by and visit tomorrow," when you know you'll be too busy tomorrow, you are engaging in a subtle form of lying.

▷ *Abandoning the act of slandering.* Slander essentially involves speaking in a way that creates discord or division between people. Suppose you wish to heal a relationship with a friend, but then you make a slightly negative or suspicious comment about that friend to someone else. As soon as the words leave your mouth, it's as though they've been posted to an Internet chat group. The person you spoke with passes the message on to everyone else in the group, and eventually the negative message is likely to reach your friend. By the time it does so, it may have been magnified many times over. On the other hand, if you maintain awareness and only say something positive and heartfelt, your friend will eventually receive a positive message. As a result, your relationship may be healed just as you intended.

▷ *Abandoning the act of using harsh words.* Bringing awareness to just this one quality of speech can change your life. Anytime you say something hurtful to a person who cares about you or to someone you depend on, you are also damaging an aspect of your own life. You risk losing a relationship, a friend, a job, a support. Conversely, when you are alert to the potential for your words to injure others and always choose gentle and kind words instead,

12. Sutra describes ten virtues in all. Beyond the four virtues of speech, the three virtues of body are abandoning the act of killing, abandoning the act of stealing, and abandoning the act of indulging in sexual misconduct; the three virtues of mind are abandoning the act of being covetous, abandoning the act of harming others, and abandoning the act of upholding wrong views or philosophies.

not only will you be speaking with enhanced awareness, you are also likely to make more friends. People who already love you will love you more. You'll receive more job offers. People will want to help you more than you need help. Sometimes unpleasant or hurtful words slip out without our realizing it when we are feeling insecure or uncomfortable. Thus, another way to avoid using harsh words is to be aware of your own state of mind and state of being.

▷ *Abandoning the act of indulging in idle gossip.* The harm of gossip or idle chatter may seem trivial. Yet, when you omit it from your daily life you will find that your speech by default is more clear, precise, direct, and meaningful, and you will experience a shift in your reality as a result. When you no longer chat in nonuseful ways, you have no choice but to speak from the heart, with more awareness. When you convey gratitude, people will know you mean it. When you talk to your children, your spouse, or your co-workers, they will automatically listen more closely and hear what you are saying.

In the monastery, monks take a vow to abandon all four forms of nonvirtuous speech. But doing so doesn't mean they have nothing left to talk about. They also engage in thoughtful debate as part of their learning process; as such, every word they say helps them to grow. When speech becomes more integrated with awareness, everything you say becomes a form of spiritual practice.

► **Engaging in prayer and mantra.** No form of speech is more virtuous than mantra, devotional prayer, and sacred seed syllables. These three forms particularly engage the spiritual practitioner in a high level of awareness, purity, and sacred intent. They empower your speech, lessen your negative energy, and bring you closer to your higher self. The words and syllables themselves may carry the divine. They allow you to connect with the presence of the master, to invoke the enlightened activity of a protector deity, or to connect deeply with your own inner wisdom. They can also be very effective in healing illness and emotions, strengthening your body's vitality, or minimizing thoughts and confusion.

▷ *Action mantra* is a language through which one communicates with the enlightened beings, guardians, and spirits. When you invoke a particular action mantra by reciting it, the being associated with that mantra becomes active. When you recite the mantra of the goddess of the earth or water element, the goddess helps to retrieve the elemental essence you need. When you recite the healing mantra of Yeshé Walmo, an important protector deity of the Tibetan Bön tradition, Yeshé Walmo offers healing. Older Tibetans commonly spend much of their day reciting mantras— and this is good if only because in cultures where mantras aren't recited, people spend their time gossiping instead. While there is often a meaning behind each of the Tibetan syllables that compose a mantra, the effect of the mantra comes very much from the syllables themselves. You recite them continuously, using the sound to develop pure, clear focus on a sacred quality within a sacred space.

▷ *Devotional prayers* are essentially poems set to melody. When you recite them, they move the heart. They help to generate devotion and to connect with the prayer's intent through the music, the words, and the meaning behind the words. Examples of devotional prayers are the guru yoga prayer, through which one connects with one's master and with the buddhas and bodhisattvas, and the bardo prayer, which one recites to help someone through the transitions of dying and death.

▷ *Seed syllables* have a very pure connection to the voidness, to the base of all. In the Bön tradition, the syllable *OM* itself is specifically associated with the throat chakra and with the quality of ceaseless speech. Yet, as pure sound, all seed syllables are related to the base and have a ceaseless quality. In this book we have already seen their use in the White Liquid Practice to Heal Disease in chapter 4. In that case, simply imagining the syllables at different chakras, or energy centers, of the body helps to awaken healing qualities, energies, and wisdom.

You can also think of the seed syllable as like an actual seed that when planted and subjected to all the right conditions will sprout, grow into a tree, and produce beneficial fruit. When you sound a specific syllable, the entire mandala of the universe can arise from it. This process is described in a commentary from the Bön *Mother Tantra*:

> From the body of the essence of the unborn arises
>   the sphere of light (tiglé).
> From that sphere of light arises wisdom.
> From wisdom arises the seed syllable.
> From the seed syllable arises (all the completion of)
>   the mandala.

From a seed syllable arises all of the mandala of the *Mother Tantra* teachings—all of the deities, divine images, divine qualities, and divine consciousnesses. Although a tree grows gradually, the transformation of a seed syllable into the divine mandala is instantaneous.

▶ **Awareness as virtue.** Beyond choosing more virtuous forms of speech, you can also try to cultivate awareness of the subtle vibration underlying your speech and of how your speech manifests from there. Is your voice creating the right energy field?

In dzogchen the concept of virtuous speech is taken to its highest level. For example, the A-Tri system of dzogchen offers a group of successive practices in which one learns to maintain awareness while engaging in various virtuous, neutral, and nonvirtuous activities. One initially tries to stay present amid virtuous activity such as praying or chanting mantras. Once that experience is stabilized, one integrates presence with neutral speech, such as conversing casually with a friend about cooking or gardening. Finally, one tries to integrate with negative speech such as lying, arguing, or giving insults. It is easier if you can establish your intent for self-awareness *before* you get drawn into an angry argument. For example, think of how courtroom lawyers argue a case: although they may use strong, sharp language, they are never driven by their emotions— every word is carefully chosen for its impact and is guided by intent, if not awareness.

From this perspective "nonvirtuous speech" might be defined as speech that is driven and not guided and through which you lose connection with your self. In dzogchen practice you aim to arrive at a place where all activity of body, speech, and mind becomes an expression of contemplative awareness and an aid to spiritual development—therefore virtuous in the truest sense of the word.

SOUND THAT INTRODUCES YOU TO PURE SPACE

Ultimately, every sound you hear, whether it's of a seed syllable, a mantra, or the wind blowing through the trees, is the sound of your own direct innate awareness. Every sound is self-arising. The question is whether you are aware of it. If you hear the wail of a siren and think "danger!" or if you hear the voice of your famous person and think "I'd rather be someplace else," that is an indication that you have not realized self-arising sound. All sounds you hear are associated with expectation, hope, or fear—even fear of silence. Therefore, they are experienced dualistically, as separate from your self.

The way to realize self-arising sound is through meditation practice, and specifically through the practice of inner sound described in chapter 8. This is a dzogchen practice that involves meditating for weeks at a time in silence with the ears blocked to avoid any distraction from external sound—just as in a dark retreat dzogchen practitioners close themselves off from all external sources of light. By meditating in complete silence, over time one is able to hear and connect nondualistically with one's inner, self-manifested sound. Eventually, with achievement of the final result, all experience of sound ceases and one realizes the voidness.

Inner sound is completely neutral. It's not the same as the sound of a friend talking, a dog barking, or a phone ringing. You are not listening to intellectual concepts and making constant judgments about them, or wondering whose dog is barking. Inner sound is the purest form of sound; it arises spontaneously from your own nature. Connecting deeply with it, being with it, allowing it to be with you, enables you to connect back to the source. Inner sound, like all sound, is a doorway to your enlightened nature because in the end it is inseparable from your enlightened nature.

Opening the Door of Speech: 6
How to Tap into Sound's Healing Potential

THE SEED SYLLABLES described in the coming chapters represent, in a pure way, your connection with your highest nature. They have great potential to heal you on many levels. Yet, if they are recited without focused attention and understanding, it is like the parrot that recites "Killing is a sin!" and then immediately gobbles up an insect. There is no real sense of what is being recited.

When you use conventional speech, you engage your conceptual thought. But when you sound the sacred warrior syllable *A*, for example, your intent is not to conceptualize but rather to connect with a pure form of energy. Someone with no sense of that energy, who identifies with pain speech and experiences mainly from the conceptual karmic body, will have difficulty connecting with the energy of *A* no matter how many times he or she recites the syllable. The power of your practice depends on your familiarity with the energy, on your sensitivity to it, and on your knowledge of its skillful use.

When you do have the right relation with the syllable as you sound it, the entire experience is one of connectedness. Consider what it is like to express heartfelt love: the sound of the words "I love you," the quality of feeling, and the sense of connection with a higher, sacred place in yourself are all intimately related. Together they form a single deep, pure expression of love.

THE EIGHT ORIGINS OF SOUND

To connect deeply with sound, you must connect all the way to its source. Each sound has a physical, energetic, and spiritual source.

The physical sources are clearly delineated in the teachings of the Bön *Mother Tantra* (*Ma Gyü*), which has classified every letter/syllable of the Tibetan alphabet according to its physical origin. As displayed in more detail in table 6.1, the eight physical origins and their associated vowels and consonants are:

Throat	*Cha Ka Kha Ga Nga*
Palate	*E Cha Ch'a Ja Nya*
Tongue	*O Ta Tha Da Na*
Lips	*U Pa Pha Ba Ma*
Nose	*I Tsa Ts'a Dza Wa*
Teeth	*Am Zha Za a Ya*
Crown	*A Ra La Sha Sa*
Stomach/Diaphragm	*Sha Ha A Bhi Ming*

The idea is that each time you use your speech, you are activating one of these specific parts of the body. Try reciting each group of syllables above, one group at a time, specifically the consonants: you can experience how each syllable originates from and vibrates the physical area indicated. In the case of the syllables of the throat, palate, tongue, and lips, the source is relatively obvious. In reciting the other syllables, you can use your imagination to connect more closely with the source.

Different seed syllables vibrate different areas of the body in the same way that a certain frequency of sound will make a wine glass vibrate. And, just as an acupuncture needle placed in one part of the body can send a healing message to a distant organ, the vibration of sound as it reverberates in the crown of your head or your diaphragm, for example, can have a strong healing effect in another area of your body.

....

TABLE 6.1 ————————————————————————————————➤

Brief Guide to Pronunciation

▶ All syllables except the vowels *O*, *U*, and *I* rhyme with the syllable *A* ("*ah*").

▶ *Zha* is pronounced like the soft "g" in "massage."

▶ The sound of *Kha* is basically *Ka* with audible breath added; this same rule applies to *Ch'a/Cha*, *Tha/Ta*, *Pha/Pa*, and *Ts'a/Tsa*.

▶ The "ng" in *Nga* is pronounced like the "ng" in "singer," a soft sound from the back of the throat.

TABLE 6.1. THE EIGHT ORIGINS OF SOUND

	Syllables				Origin	Element	Animal	Khandro	Path
Cha (ksha)	Ka	Kha	Ga	Nga	Throat	Wood	Tiger, Rabbit	8 Cemetery Khandros	Path of accumulation
E	Cha	Ch'a	Ja	Nya	Palate	Fire	Horse, Snake	4 Consort Khandros	Path of preparation
O	Ta	Tha	Da	Na	Tongue	Earth	Sheep	24 locational Khandros	Path of seeing
U	Pa	Pha	Ba	Ma	Lips	Water	Rat, Pig	6 guardian Khandros	Path of meditation
I	Tsa	Ts'a	Dza	Wa	Nose	Air	Dragon	4 Khandros	Path of freedom
Am	Zha	Za	a	Ya	Teeth	Metal	Rooster, Monkey	4 Khandros	Path of liberation
A	Ra	La	Sha	Sa	Crown	Mountain	Ox		
Sha	Ha	A	Bhi	Ming	Stomach/diaphragm	Space	Dog		

Source: Bön Mother Tantra (Ma Gyü)

The right sounds can help balance the five elements of earth, water, fire, air, and space, with subtle but potent effects on your physical, mental, and spiritual states.

Notice, too, that in each case the root sound of the consonants is the seed syllable *A* (*"ah"*). *A* is the soul of all the consonants. It represents Samantabhadra, the dharmakaya, the wisdom of emptiness, the center, ceaseless arising, the birthless state, clear light. Sounding *A* is a way to connect deeply with all that *A* represents. Every letter of the Tibetan alphabet can be traced to its source in *A* and the rest of the five warrior seed syllables—and through those five sacred syllables to the five wisdoms and ultimately to space itself.[13]

How to Connect through Sound

Nothing could seem easier and more relaxing than reciting *A* in a long, drawn-out way, over and over. But how do you bring your mind to the right place with the sound? Here are some things to be aware of before engaging in sound practice:

1. While reciting, you will first want to feel the vibration at the place of the sound's physical origin, whether the palate, tongue, or—as in the practice of the five warrior syllables—the specific chakra you are working with. By drawing your awareness to the place of vibration, you are connecting with and activating the prana.[14] The vibration has the ability to transform and move things within you. It has the ability to dissipate the prana that holds the physical blocks, energetic or emotional disturbances, and mental obscurations. Feel the opening that comes as these obstacles are cleared.

2. While sounding, also experience a quality of light, of illumination, that radiates with the sound of the seed syllable. Many seed syllables have a specific color; for example, in some practices *OM* is seen as a luminous red, *HUNG* as a luminous blue, and *DZA* as a luminous green. As the vibration dissipates the obscurations held

---

13. For more about the five warrior syllables, see chapter 7.

14. Prana is discussed in more detail in chapter 12, "Mind and Prana in Meditation Practice." See also my book *Healing with Form, Energy and Light: The Five Elements in Tibetan Shamanism, Tantra, and Dzogchen* (Ithaca, N.Y.: Snow Lion Publications, 2002), chap. 3.

by the prana, experience that this light is dissipating the obscurations held by the mind.

3. The powerful clearing effect of vibration and light brings a greater sense of openness. Through that openness you can now connect more easily with the specific quality associated with the seed syllable. For example, *OM* has the quality of spontaneity—when sounding *OM*, because the light and vibration have dissipated the obstacles to your connecting with spontaneity, that quality can now more freely arise within you. When sounding *HUNG*, you are able to experience the quality of flexibility because the light and vibration have cleared the obstacles to flexibility.

4. Finally, maintaining this sense of openness and connection with the quality opens a doorway for you to connect more easily with the space that is the primary source from which all sound arises. That deeper wisdom quality, which is the embodiment of light and space, is what you ultimately wish to realize. In the end, you want to be self-aware. No matter what other outcomes are intended from the practice, the experience of space is always the same.

To summarize, you will want to connect clearly with the sound of the syllable, with its field of energy and vibration, with its luminosity, with its quality, and ultimately with the space from which sound arises. Feel awareness in that space and be in that space.

Not everyone can connect right away with the deeper experiences. If you can't be in the space, at least connect with the quality. And if you can't connect with the quality, at least have the awareness of the physical location and of the sound and its vibration. That awareness has a beneficial effect in itself.

LETTING GO

When you recite the healing sound *HIK*, you are soothing a headache. When you sound *PHET!*, you are directly cutting through a negative emotion or other obstacle. When you sound *OM* in the Five-Warrior-Syllables Practice, you are cultivating the quality of spontaneous perfection. Each time you sound a syllable it seems as though you are working at making something happen. However, when it comes to the actual practice, try not to put too much effort into forcing something to happen. Instead, just relax, allow the result, and be aware of the result.

It is true that you need to learn the right way to sound the syllable, its correct location and color, and how to connect. But if you try to force a result, your conceptual mind is already occupying the very space you are trying to clear. This is like trying to clear everything out of your house through the front door even as more furniture is being brought in through the back: you won't achieve the desired result.

In both dzogchen and the higher tantras, it is agreed that there is no way to experience space, the essence, the ultimate wisdom, through intellectual means alone. The more you think and analyze, the less likely it is that you will have the experience that is beyond all concepts and dualistic thinking. When you connect with sound, you are preparing all the causes and conditions, then releasing all intellectual effort and just being. There is more presence of space in that experience.

Letting go of familiar patterns, even negative ones, can be challenging, and just a glimpse of the vast space within you can make you fearful. When you actually connect with the changelessness of the essence, you naturally become fearless and confident. But since this process is so unfamiliar, it helps to rely on the power of prayer. You can open your heart and pray to all the masters with whom you have a direct or indirect connection and to all the beings from the past, present, and future who are your inspiration. You can ask them: "Please empower me, bless me to overcome these fears and doubts and to recognize and connect more with this unchanging, vast, fearless space." You can also pray that the specific innate quality you most need will be revealed. Then you can trust that the sound has the power to give you direct access to deep qualities such as wisdom, spontaneity, flexibility, love, or joy.

When your prayer is accompanied by a strong desire for the result, it can immediately unblock the obscuring conditions. It can also eventually allow you to recognize the space. Praying for a physical result, such as overcoming disease or buying a new house, will not necessarily awaken you to something internally. But here in the sound practice you are praying to connect with the nature of mind. You are praying from a deep place and touching not only the problem—your fear of space—but also the enlightened beings who embody and support the result. As you pray, your immediate fear is removed on a gross level because you are truly engaged with the support. But the prayer also awakens something on a subtle level of the mind, which remains with you throughout your practice even as you are no longer conceptually engaging with the support. It's similar to praying before going to sleep at night, asking a deity to remove your fear of the dark. Not only is your immediate fear removed, but the deity may also appear in your dreams to help you all night long.

The teachings say that the buddhas are always there to tirelessly help all sentient beings. They help effortlessly and spontaneously—but without any desire or plan of action. Why would the buddhas help if they have no desire to do so? It is because they prayed while on the path to enlightenment: "When I achieve liberation, may I help all sentient beings," and their prayers have been realized. In the same way, you can pray at the beginning of your meditation, let go of all your plans to do things right, and just be open to the power of the higher beings to bring your mind to the right place as you connect with the sacred syllables.

The Five Indestructible Warrior Sounds: 7
The Essence of the Five Wisdoms

The seed syllables are the fighters of demons,
therefore they are warriors.
They are the essence of the five wisdoms.
They are the antidote to the five poisons.
They are the mudra of the body of the five deities.
They are these five: quality, action,
body, speech, and mind.

—FROM *ZER MIG*, THE MEDIUM-LENGTH
BIOGRAPHY OF TÖNPA SHENRAB

B EFORE THE DEVELOPMENT of human language, before the sound
of the *A–Li* vowels and the *Ka–Li* consonants, there were only
the sounds of nature: waterfalls, wind, rain. Sound had no conceptual
associations. When we trace sound farther back to its very beginnings,
we arrive at the pure, primordial sounds of the seed syllables.

According to the ancient Bön Buddhist tradition, the first sounds that
arose from the essence were the five warrior seed syllables, the *pawo
dru nga* (*pawo*, "warrior"; *dru*, "seed"; *nga*, "five"). As the quotation
suggests, they are called warriors because they have the ability to conquer our demons. The demons they fight are not necessarily evil beings;
rather, they are the familiar demons of our emotions from which the
experience of evil may arise. There are four other classes of demons
mentioned in the teachings, some related to karmic forces, others to
the subtlest attachment of our own grasping mind (see appendix 3).
Whether we are troubled by distracting thoughts, having problems

with anger, feeling too much desire or attachment, or suffering from karma-related chronic illness, whatever obstacle or obscuration we have is related to one of these demons. And for every demon, there is a warrior syllable that can overcome it.

The warrior syllables are pure and indestructible. They are able to penetrate through fear and cannot be destroyed by it. They cut through ignorance and open space; they are the doorway to connecting back to the original essence and to the wisdom qualities that arise from the essence.

The five warrior syllables are the seed syllables of the five wisdoms.[15] According to Tibetan Bön Buddhism, the profound empathy of compassion is not enough to bring us to enlightenment; there must also be wisdom. Only wisdom can ultimately destroy the deluded ego that is the source of all our demons.

THE INTERNAL WARRIOR SYLLABLES

For several years now I have been teaching a practice of the five internal warrior seed syllables, *A, OM, HUNG, RAM,* and *DZA,* based on a text from an oral transmission of the fourteenth century called *The Peaceful Luminous A (Zhiwa A Sel).* These five are the focus of this chapter and the guided practice with the five warrior sounds in the next chapter. However, there are two other sets of five warrior seed syllables. The biography of Tönpa Shenrab (*Zi Ji,* the long version, from the Bön Kangyur, Oral Transmission of *loden nyingpo*) says:

> From the mandala of the hearts of the five deities
> radiate the lights of the five wisdoms,
> *KAM, YAM, RAM, SUM,* and *OM;*
> *A, OM, HUNG, RAM,* and *DZA;*
> *SO, UM, HUNG, HE,* and *BHYO;*
> [which are] the external, internal,
> and secret warrior [seed syllables].

15. See the description of the five wisdoms in chapter 11 on the *Ma Gyü* Mandala.

All three sets of warrior syllables—external, internal, and secret—comprise important original mantras (see table 7.1). The internal warrior syllables are already familiar to many practitioners of the Tibetan spiritual traditions. For example, in guru yoga practice, *A*, *OM*, and *HUNG* are visualized or sounded to help empower the practitioner with enlightened body, speech, and mind.[16] Tibetan lamas inscribe these same three syllables on sacred images and reliquaries such as paintings, photographs, and large stupas to empower and authenticate them. Without that authentication, a photographic print is no more than paper, and a thangka wall hanging is just cloth.

TABLE 7.1. THE FIVE INTERNAL WARRIOR SYLLABLES

Syllable	What it represents	Chakra location	Color	Element	Wisdom	Deity
A	Body	Crown	White	Space	Wisdom of emptiness	Khagying Karpo
OM	Speech	Throat	Yellow	Earth	Mirrorlike wisdom	Mugyung Karpo
HUNG	Mind	Heart	Green	Air	Wisdom of equanimity	Muyang Déwo
RAM	Quality	Navel	Red	Fire	Discriminating wisdom	Musang Gungyel
DZA	Action	Secret chakra	Blue	Water	All-accomplishing wisdom	Mumé Thayé

Source: *The Peaceful Luminous A (Zhiwa A Sel)*, a text from an oral transmission of the fourteenth century

16. Most traditions of Bön associate the syllable *A* with enlightened body and the crown chakra; *OM* with enlightened speech and the throat chakra; and *HUNG* with enlightened mind and the heart chakra. However, in the major Tibetan Buddhist schools as well as some Bön traditions, *A* and *OM* are reversed: *OM* is correlated with enlightened body and the crown, *A* with enlightened speech and the throat.

In the Bön Buddhist tradition, inscribing *A* on an image in red ink activates body and creates space within the image. Inscribing *OM* activates speech and all the enlightened qualities, such as love and compassion. Inscribing *HUNG* activates the heart/mind and the ability to radiate and manifest those qualities. Once fully empowered, the image is said to embody the actual body, speech, and mind of the deity.

The fourth and fifth warrior syllables are *RAM*, the seed syllable of the fire element, and *DZA*, the seed syllable of action. These two have a particularly powerful, active quality and are sometimes included with *A*, *OM* and *HUNG* when authenticating certain images.

In meditation practice, voicing these five syllables in progression

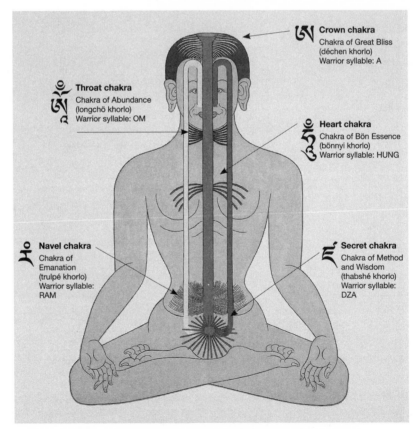

Figure 7.1 The three channels, five chakras, and five warrior
seed syllables (see also plate 5)

enables us to connect through the sound in a pure, direct way with higher states of being. Sounding them helps us to connect with the clear, open, primordially pure space that is the base of all, and then in turn to experience, and ultimately manifest, the enlightened qualities we most need.

Through the five warrior syllables, we are able to effect profound shifts in our experience and awareness, with life-changing implications. These syllables are almost unbelievably powerful. In fact, many people *don't* believe in their power. Reciting them seems too easy—and if a practice is easy, it may seem less interesting.

TABLE 7.2 PRONUNCIATION GUIDE

A	Pronounced "ah," like the "a" sound in the word *calm*
OM	Rhymes with *home*
HUNG	The "u" sounds like the "oo" in *book*
RAM	The "a" sounds like the "a" in *calm*
DZA	Sharp and percussive; the front upper and lower teeth come together, with the tongue pressing against them as you sharply release the "dz" sound into the "ah" sound like the "a" in the word *calm*

THE MEANING OF EACH SYLLABLE

When working with the warrior syllables, it is important to understand the qualities each one represents:

A **is the sound of space.** It is the sound of the essence, of unbounded openness, of the changeless state of awareness and being. It has an aspect of clearing. *A* is self-originated and primordially pure. Its color is clear, luminous white, and its location is the crown chakra, the chakra of great bliss. As *A* is sounded, its vibration emanates from the crown and the place of the third eye (between and just above the eyebrows), opening space and clearing all obstacles and obscurations. It can clear away fear, emotion, any karmic condition, any of the demons. It opens up the profound space that is already there in us.

When you are able to connect through *A* to the base of all, the experience is like sitting on a mountaintop under a vast, crystal-clear sky overlooking a vast desert. If you can go deep enough into that experience of space and then continue to abide there without changing, without elaborating, the experience can ripen in you. When it does, you become fearless. You develop the *confidence of changelessness*, the confidence of the changeless precious body. Just as change is the source of fear, changelessness is the source of confidence. Attaining confidence in the changeless view of *A* is like receiving the initiation of dharmakaya.

OM is the sound of infinite, ceaseless quality. "Quality" refers here to all the perfected virtues of enlightened beings: the quality of compassion is perfected in *OM*, as are joy, love, equanimity, generosity, openness, and peacefulness. If you were to associate *OM* with just one specific quality, it would be compassion. Wisdom is the space, and compassion is the quality that arises from the space. The ceaseless quality of *OM* is not manifested; rather, it exists as a state of unlimited potential and spontaneous perfection (*lhündrup*) like the sun shining in a clear, cloudless sky. Sounding *OM* brings one to a sense of fullness, completeness, where nothing is lacking. *OM* is luminous red, and its location is the throat chakra—the chakra of abundance, associated with one's entire sense of being.

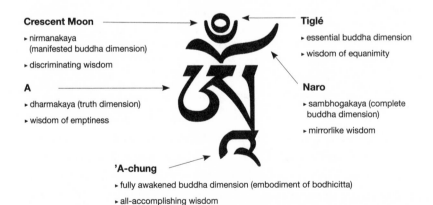

Crescent Moon
- nirmanakaya (manifested buddha dimension)
- discriminating wisdom

A
- dharmakaya (truth dimension)
- wisdom of emptiness

Tiglé
- essential buddha dimension
- wisdom of equanimity

Naro
- sambhogakaya (complete buddha dimension)
- mirrorlike wisdom

'A-chung
- fully awakened buddha dimension (embodiment of bodhicitta)
- all-accomplishing wisdom

Figure 7.2 The five wisdoms and kayas of the seed syllable *OM*. Of the five warrior syllables, *OM* is particularly rich in symbolism. Each of its five calligraphic elements is said to embody one of the five kayas/dimensions and the five wisdoms.

HUNG **is the sound of manifestation.** As you recite this syllable, feel a specific quality vividly and distinctly, emanating out like the rays of the sun shining in a clear, cloudless sky over a vast desert. The quality you work with depends on your needs. Feel the compassion, joy, love, or equanimity and its connection to the clear, unchanging space and the pure, unceasing energy. This quality is no longer just a state of potential; it now has form, appearance, and fullness of presence. *HUNG* is luminous blue, and its location is the heart chakra—the chakra of bön essence. Through *HUNG* one can attain undeluded confidence.

RAM **is the sound of active quality.** *RAM* is the seed syllable of the fire element. When sounding *RAM*, that one quality you most need is now highly activated, fully ripened, perfected, and ready to manifest. It may be ready to emerge as laughter, joy, creativity, or a sense of helping yourself or others. Its color is luminous red, and its location is the navel chakra—the chakra of emanation.

DZA **is the sound of action.** When sounding *DZA*, the quality you are cultivating spontaneously manifests into your room, your home, the entire environment, the universe, where it satisfies the needs of all beings and removes their suffering. You feel a continuous connection to the changeless space, the unceasing pure vibration, and the undiluted active quality. You merge with and are active in the energy of this light. *DZA* is luminous green, and its location is the secret chakra in the area of the sexual organs—the chakra of method and wisdom.

▶ ——————————————————————————————

The Five Warrior Syllables

A

Sing again and again the self-originated sound of *A*.
Radiate luminous white light from the forehead chakra.
The secret karmic obscurations dissolve at the source,
Clear and open like a cloudless desert sky.
Abide without changing or elaborating.
All fears are overcome

And changeless confidence is attained.
May I experience the wisdom of emptiness.

OM

Sing again and again the self-clear sound of OM.
Radiate luminous red light from the throat chakra.
All knowledge and experiences of the Four Immeasurables
Arise like sunshine in the clear, cloudless sky.
Abiding there: clear, radiant, complete,
All conditions of hope are overcome
And ceaseless confidence is attained.
May I experience mirrorlike wisdom.

HUNG

Sing again and again the nondual sound of *HUNG*.
Radiate luminous blue light from the heart chakra.
The wisdom heat of the Four Immeasurables
Pervades like sunlight in all directions.
From nondual wisdom, allow the quality you need to radiate.
All distortions of doubt are overcome
And undeluded confidence is attained.
May I experience the wisdom of equanimity.

RAM

Sing again and again the ripening sound of *RAM*.
Radiate luminous red light from the navel chakra.
All the enlightened qualities that one needs
Ripen like fruit in the warmth of the sun.
Meditating on these spontaneously arising virtues
The demons of conflicting emotions are overcome
And ripened confidence is attained.
May I experience discriminating-awareness wisdom.

DZA

Sing again and again the sound of action, the syllable *DZA*.
Radiate luminous green light from the secret chakra

To all beings who suffer and are in need.
Just as a good harvest satisfies hunger,
The Four Immeasurables bring happiness and freedom.
External obstacles are overcome
And effortless confidence is attained.
May I experience all-accomplishing wisdom.

© 2007 Tenzin Wangyal Rinpoche

Understanding the Progression

As you can see, when you progress from one syllable and chakra to the next—from crown, to throat, heart, navel, and secret chakra—the more defined the quality becomes. The experience begins with space and becomes grosser and grosser until it becomes full, active manifestation.

To better understand this progression, imagine that you have a beautiful expanse of open land. It is like space, like *A*, vast, pure, and unchanging.

There is infinite potential to create anything you want or need on that piece of land. This state of unceasing, unlimited potential, in the space where nothing has yet manifested, is like *OM*, spontaneous perfection. You could keep the land as an open space lit up by the sky; you could create a sacred temple with fragrant gardens; you could build a house with the warm, protective quality of home; or you could erect a place of business. This unlimited potential is experienced as a sense of completeness and fullness.

Now, imagine that you come up with a blueprint for what will be specifically created on the land. You may clearly envision a home there. The space is still there, the infinite potential is still there, but some kind of design has manifested from that space to respond to your needs and conditions. You experience the fullness of presence of one of the qualities, such as compassion, love, openness, or joy. This is *HUNG*, the nascent manifestation.

In the next stage, your home is well into construction and poised for completion. By now, you have decided on the color of the cabinets and the kitchen sink and may have already sent out invitations for your open house celebration. This is like the active quality of *RAM*. The space no longer hosts just the potential for all the enlightened qualities, nor is it just a blueprint for one of them: now it has also a fully ripened, perfected, vivid quality of joy, love, or compassion, whichever quality you need most.

And now comes *DZA*—the action, the active manifestation. The house is built, the drywall is painted, pictures are hung, comfortable, attractive furniture is in place. Friends and family arrive for the open house, everyone is laughing and chatting, the lamps glow, birds sing in the trees, children play, the sunshine is warm and nourishing. When your love, joy, peacefulness, or some other quality fully and actively manifests, everything you experience, both inwardly and outwardly, reflects that quality.

If you walk into a joyful person's room, you clearly see the manifestation of joy there. If you spend a weekend with a joyful person, you receive little rays of joy from them all weekend. By connecting with *DZA*, you yourself can be that joyful person. As you sound it, imagine that you radiate the light of joy, equanimity, compassion, or love to whomever you encounter.

The guided practice "A Practice with the Five Warrior Sounds" (chapter 8) shows how you can work with *A*, *OM*, *HUNG*, *RAM*, and *DZA* to connect deeply and fully with all these experiences, including the experience of manifestation. During the practice session, you are not jumping off your meditation cushion and building a house or otherwise interacting with the external world. But while sounding the syllables, you clearly feel the quality as manifesting through all your thoughts and senses. Think of a mother who has lost her children and then finds them—how much intensity of joy she will feel. Think of someone who has just won the lottery, or a person who has just been released after many years in prison. As you sound *DZA*, the practice can bring this same sense of freedom, joy, and creativity.

If you actually act on those feelings, your actions will be very positive. Why? Because your actions will be defined on the basis of pure space and unceasing energy and awareness. Conditional joy or conditional love is based on feelings of ownership, attachment, or identification. Absolute joy, on the other hand, has no conditions. It is your deep connection to the space in which you feel joy. Absolute love is your connection with the space from which love arises.

CHANGING OUR KARMIC PATTERNS

With the space of *A* and the infinite potential of *OM* always accessible, what happens in day-to-day life can be magical. We can be anything: we can be happy, joyful, open, generous. All of these qualities, all of this beauty and perfection, are within us. The reason we haven't realized them, the reason they don't manifest in our life, is because something is blocking that space. If clear, open space is not there, the quality will not manifest. So, space is fundamental. Qualities are very much dependent on our connection with space.

When there is no such connection to space, then despite all our desires for happiness and all our good intentions, we continue to follow specific patterns of delusion in the way we live our lives. We are like a piece of rolled-up paper that when opened always tries to return to its original form: we want to act in a loving manner, but as soon as someone disrespects us, we get angry. We want to feel balanced and grounded, but as soon as we get stuck in traffic, we immediately get flustered and confused. The opportunity to be loving or grounded is always there, but we always seem to return to our karmic patterns. What's more, usually we don't discover the opportunity to be loving until after we've been driven into an angry, hurtful argument. At the decisive moment, the road to anger seems direct and obvious; the signs pointing to love and compassion are much more subtle.

If space is clear, energy is clear. If space is not clear, energy is not clear. When working with *A*, we want to clear the space as much as possible so that what arises from it is as pure as possible.

Changing our karmic patterns requires not only clear space and awareness but also taking time to cultivate the desired quality. I find that it is a weakness of Western practitioners that they tend to engage a lot in purification practice—clearing what is negative—but very little in cultivation. As a result, they often fall back into their karmic patterns because the quality has not been permitted to develop and mature.

The ability to change focus is also critical. If something terrible happened to you ten years ago, must you hold onto it today? The answer is clearly no. But how do you change your focus? You could try to change the way your emotions manifest—such as treating your famous person kindly instead of lashing out in anger. But instead of forcing the result, a better place for a change in focus might be in the cause itself.

If you create the right space, the right energy will come. Once the right energy is there, you can take the time to set up the conditions that will allow love, joy, or some other quality to take form in your perception. Then you can permit that quality to manifest.

MANIFESTATION PRACTICE

Entering into a deep meditation on love or compassion feels good and continued practice in a protective, supportive environment is essential to becoming familiar with a quality and cultivating it. Yet, when we reenter our daily lives and face the realities of difficult clients, stressful traffic, or money problems, we can have a lot of resistance to actually manifesting love, joy, or equanimity.

Putting *DZA* into action in daily life can loosen up our resistance. Doing so requires courage and openness since it goes against the grain of our normal karmic patterns. But it's important to take that action because it will result in so much change.

A student of mine told me how she had once lost an important, close friendship with a girlfriend because of a petty argument. As a result they stopped talking for several years. But after doing the practice with the warrior syllables, she was moved to communicate with her friend and sent her an e-mail. Her friend went online, saw the message waiting, and immediately sent back a response: "I haven't even read your message yet, but I'm so happy to hear from you!" The simple act of sending an e-mail brought an immediate reconnection and healed the relationship.

Another student of mine from Poland had a difficult relationship with his stepmother for close to twenty years. After he started doing the warrior syllables practice, his stepmother was hospitalized with an illness. By then he had gained enough openness, clarity, and courage to take steps to heal their relationship, and for the first time in his life, he was able to give her a hug. He told me he experienced an incredible release after decades of feeling blocked.

Unless you feel you need to take action and then make specific plans to do so, you are unlikely to experience this kind of transformation. The only action needed to heal a relationship may be to pick up the phone or attach a stamp to a postcard. Still, doing so can require openness, courage, compassion, and kindness.

WHERE TO START

When beginning your own "manifestation practice," how do you know where to start? Consider that everyone has at least one of three kinds of relationships in his or her life:

- *External relationships* in one's professional life—with colleagues, one's boss, or other business contacts
- *Internal relationships* in one's home life—with one's partner or other family members
- *Sacred relationships* in one's spiritual life—with one's teacher or sangha members

You can reflect on these three areas and try to determine which one is most important for you to concentrate on right now. If you are having difficulties at work, your practice might involve bringing a sense of awareness into your professional life or introducing to it some understanding of love, joy, equanimity, or compassion. It is possible to feel strong, pure, clear, and loving while entering computer data, talking with customers or coworkers, hauling lumber, designing architectural plans, or writing reports. The point is that you do not have to lose a precious quality while you are earning money for material needs.

Improvements in one area of your life can be the basis for improvements in all other areas. If business is thriving, monetary wealth can be translated into feelings of abundance in one's marriage. Equanimity cultivated through working with difficult customers can also be applied when your child misbehaves. Feelings of satisfaction and personal power gained during the workday can help to nurture and heal personal relationships at home in the evening.

A strong, loving relationship with your family, in turn, can help you nurture a higher relationship with your spiritual family—with the sangha, the teacher, and the teachings.

Whether in meditation practice or manifestation practice, cultivating one of the immeasurable qualities of love, joy, equanimity, or compassion is the doorway to finding your true self, which is the openness of space and light and the center of the mandala.

In the end, it's all about who you are. Because you have connected with the space within and cultivated and manifested the quality, you are a good being. You can transmit love or joy to everyone you relate to. As a result, a positive energy is created in all your relationships and perhaps even in your entire community.

Practices of Speech **8**

T his chapter includes a variety of sound-related practices from the Tibetan Bön Buddhist tradition. The first guided meditation allows you to put into practice the knowledge of the five warrior syllables just discussed. Next, a section on "Healing Sounds" describes how to use certain syllables for targeted healing of physical maladies, energetic disturbances, or obscurations of mind. The *A Li Ka Li* mantra and the Healing Practice of Chétak Ngomé directly purify speech through a mantra composed of all the vowels and consonants of the Tibetan alphabet. Finally, there is an explanation of how to connect with sound in the subtlest and deepest manner possible through a practice with *inner sound*.

A Practice with the Five Warrior Sounds: Using Primordial Sounds to Abide in the Nature

This is a relatively simple yet powerful practice that makes use of the primordial warrior sounds to bring you to a state of abiding in the nature of mind. This practice comes from *The Peaceful Luminous A (Zhiwa A Sel)*, a text from an oral transmission of the fourteenth century.

Outwardly the core practice is simple, as it only involves reciting the five warrior syllables in succession, but the instructions for preparation are a bit more complex. You will have the best results by reading in advance this entire explanation as well as chapters 6 and 7. Then, move on to the practice, sound a syllable, and let go of all the details you've read. Relax as fully, deeply, and openly as possible into the experience of the sound. Later you can refer back to the instructions to refresh your understanding.

What to Think about Beforehand

Before doing the Five-Warrior-Syllables Practice, it is helpful to do the following:

- ▶ **Think about your obstacles.** Call to mind a problem that has been consistently arising in your life—an obstacle that is clearly recognizable to you and that may affect several areas of your life, such as your work, personal relationships, or spiritual development. Do you regularly find yourself in conflict with certain people? Does a specific negative emotion always keep arising? Do you often face the same obstacle to meditation practice, such as an agitated or dull mind?

- ▶ **Decide which quality you need to work with.** Choose the one quality that would serve as the best antidote for the obstacle or obscuration you need to clear. I recommend you begin by choosing one of the four immeasurable qualities of love, joy, equanimity, or compassion. For example, love can be an antidote to anger, joy an antidote to sadness or depression, equanimity an antidote to emotional instability, and compassion an antidote to a strong ego. Other qualities that you can cultivate that may serve as antidotes include peacefulness, openness, generosity, and a sense of security, anything that you feel will best address the problem you want to clear.

- ▶ **Remember the purpose in sounding each syllable.** *The purpose of sounding A* is to open and connect with space. Visualize all your obstacles as being cleared, particularly the one obstacle that gives you the greatest problem. *The purpose of sounding OM* is to experience and connect with the qualities arising from that space. Allow all the unceasing, spontaneously perfected qualities to arise, such as love, joy, equanimity, and compassion. In particular, experience the specific quality you most need. *The purpose of sounding HUNG, RAM,* and *DZA* is to manifest the needed quality (see the detailed instructions within the guided practice below). In a simplified version of the practice you can sound only *A*, *OM*, and *HUNG*, in which case *HUNG* will also incorporate the highly active quality of *RAM* and the fully activated manifestation of *DZA*.

Before entering the practice it is important to keep in mind that both the clear space and the quality already exist within you; it is not a matter of creating them but of recognizing their presence. For example, sounding *A* clears the sadness that keeps you from recognizing the space that is there, and connecting with the space in turn permits you, while sounding *OM*, to recognize the joy that already exists in the space. If an energetic block remains, however, when you sound *OM*, you will not experience the arising and manifestation of joy.

Practice the *tsa lung* movements, if you wish. This physical meditation practice helps to open the chakras used in the warrior syllables practice and permits the free flow of energy through them. Right before doing the warrior syllables practice, you can do three repetitions of the life-force prana exercise described in chapter 14 or one each of the five physical tsa lung practices as described in my book *Awakening the Sacred Body*.[17]

▶ **Know the right connection with sound.** Before you sing each syllable, connect with the space within the chakra, feel the presence of the light of awareness there, and realize the inseparability of the space and light. Once you feel this connection, feel the vibration and the existence of the sound within the silence and allow it to transform into physical sound as you begin to sing the seed syllable. Sing in a continuous, full, resonating tone, feeling the vibration deep within the chakra. You want to connect very clearly with the syllable's sound, luminosity, field of energy, and vibration, and the space from which it arises. Feel awareness in that space and be in that space. Although the outcome of sounding each syllable is different, the experience of space is always the same.

▶ **Be aware of the gaze.** The practices can be done with eyes open or

17. Tenzin Wangyal Rinpoche, *Awakening the Sacred Body*, ed. Marcy Vaughn (Carlsbad, Calif.: Hay House, 2011).

with eyes closed to reduce distractions. When singing *A* with eyes open, an upward gaze is helpful in order to experience more space. For *OM*, use a level gaze. With *HUNG, RAM*, and *DZA*, tilt your neck slightly down, tuck in your chin while keeping the spine straight, and gaze slightly downward for a more concentrated, focused, grounded gaze to further substantiate the manifestation. Gaze into space without focusing on any object, toward a location about sixteen finger-widths from your eyes.

▶ **Rely on imagery.** Just as an image in a dream completes the expression of feelings you had while falling asleep, the visualization of being on a mountaintop beneath a crystal clear, vast sky, for example, can complete your experience of space and openness in meditation practice.

▶ **Go deep into the practice.** You can sing each syllable several times over for just a minute or two, or you can continuously sing it for twenty minutes or longer. The deeper you go, the more powerful the practice will be.

The Five-Warrior-Syllables Practice

▶ Assume the five-point meditation posture (see chapter 4). Relax and find your center.

▶ In the clear sky in front of you, imagine a circle of rainbow light. In the center of the rainbow is a clear, luminous, naked being, Samantabhadra (Tib. Kuntuzangpo), who represents the union of all the masters with whom you have direct or indirect connection and all the beings who are your inspiration, from the past, present, and future. This single luminous being represents all of them and especially your direct master. With open, pure devotion, pray to this being: "Please purify me of all my negative karma and perfect me with all the virtues and wisdom qualities." Visualize and feel that purifying light comes down, blessing and empowering you. As you pray, feel the qualities of this being within you. Feel that you are one with the essence of the master.

▶ Perform the physical tsa lung movements, if you know them.

▶ Reflect on whatever obstacles, energetic blocks or mental obscurations disturb your connection to yourself. Feel them in your body, feel the energetic character of these disturbances, and become aware of any images or thoughts associated with them.

▶ *Draw your attention to the crown chakra*, then specifically to the forehead, the place of the third eye. Pray to the being above you to bless you in overcoming your fear of releasing your obstacles and of encountering the vast space that is your own essence.

▶ Connect with the primordially pure space in that chakra. Then connect with the light of awareness in that space. From the inseparable space and awareness feel, imagine, or visualize the seed syllable *A*, white and luminous. *A* is the sound of pure space, the **unchanging body**.

▶ As you sing the sound *A* again and again, imagine the presence of luminous white light in your forehead. Feel that the sound, vibration, and light are opening and clearing all the obstacles, especially the obstacle that is most affecting you. Feel the presence of space more and more, as if sitting on a mountaintop under the vast, crystal-clear sky, overlooking a vast desert. Feel that through the power of your meditation and the blessings, whatever obscures you becomes clearer and clearer and any problems dissipate.

Sound *A* three times:
A A A

▶ Abide in the space of openness. Recognize yourself there, as a lost son recognizes his mother in a crowd. Feel the fearlessness, the changelessness. Feel like a warrior. Rest in this experience.

▶ *Gradually draw attention to the throat chakra.* Pray to the luminous being: "Please give me the power to overcome hopes and doubts and empower me to connect to the unceasing qualities that are within me at this very moment."

► Connect to the primordially pure space at this chakra. Then, connect with the light, the awareness. From the inseparable space and light, feel, imagine, or visualize the presence of *OM*, red and luminous.

► Continuously sound *OM*. As you do, visualize, feel, and hear the red *OM* syllable emanating from the throat. Imagine that the sound and vibration of *OM* are like the bright sun shining in the clear, open sky over the vast desert. Through the ceaseless qualities of the light and energy, connect with all the enlightened qualities such as compassion, love, joy, and equanimity and especially connect with the quality you most need.

► Feel the unceasing energy, the spontaneous perfection, the unlimited potential, the pure connection to the quality. Connect with **unceasing speech** through *OM*.

  Sound *OM* three times:
  OM OM OM

► Abide in a sense of fullness, where nothing is missing and nothing is lacking. It is complete as it is.

► *Gradually draw your attention to the heart chakra.* Pray from this deep place for blessings to manifest the full presence of the quality you most need in your life, such as one of the four immeasurables.

► Connect to the primordially pure space at this chakra. Then connect with the light of awareness. From the inseparable space and light, feel, imagine, or visualize the presence of *HUNG*, blue and luminous in your heart. *HUNG* represents **undeluded mind** and supports you to embody the quality you need. Allow yourself to feel that quality as strongly as possible in your heart, clear, direct, vivid, and real through every sense. As you sing *HUNG*, whatever blocks you from abiding in the full presence of this immeasurable quality is dissolved in the space.

Sound *HUNG* three times:
HUNG HUNG HUNG

▸ Abide in the fullness of *presence with the quality.*

▸ *Gradually draw your attention to the navel chakra.* Pray: "Please help me to release all obstacles, blocks, and mental obscurations that veil this immeasurable quality so that it may fully ripen in me and may find a place and location to manifest in my life." Ask for blessings that enable you to feel this quality in particular situations, toward a particular person, and especially at the moment you feel you are weak and driven by your anger or blocks. Pray that the quality will come spontaneously through the blessings of the masters and enlightened beings and the power of your practice and awareness.

▸ Connect to the primordially pure space in this chakra. Then connect with the light of awareness. From the inseparable space and light, feel, imagine, or visualize the presence of *RAM*, red and luminous. As you sound *RAM* over and over, feel that the quality is ripening fully as you connect with the **perfected quality**. Feel the experience extending to all your life relationships.

Sound *RAM* three times:
RAM RAM RAM

▸ Abide in the fullness and perfection of the quality and a sense of *connecting with other.*

▸ *Gradually draw your attention to the secret chakra, the chakra of manifestation.* Pray to the figure above to help you fully manifest the quality that is perfected in you to specific people, places, and situations, and at specific times and in specific ways. Pray that the quality manifests naturally, spontaneously, and effortlessly.

▸ First connect with the primordially pure space at this chakra. Then connect with the light of awareness. From the inseparable space and light, feel, imagine, or visualize the green luminous DZA, the seed syllable of action. Continuously sing *DZA*. As you do, imagine that through the sound, vibration, and green light of *DZA*, the one quality you most need fully, actively manifests in **spontaneous action**. Feel the quality manifesting through your skin, bones, internal organs, senses, thoughts, emotions, energy, and mental images. Feel and see *DZA* spread from deep within your heart, like rays of sunshine, into the entire open sky and all corners of the universe, pervading every aspect of your life: every place, every person you have a connection with, all the environment, all sentient beings. Feel and see these rays reflected back to you from all experience.

Sound *DZA* three times:
DZA DZA DZA

► Feel the spontaneous great bliss of confidence. Abide in the fullness of the *quality with action.*

► Seal the merit of your practice by dedicating it to the enlightenment of all sentient beings.

► After the last syllable has been sounded, feel how wonderful it would be to actually take action as an extension of these practices. For example, if you practice with the quality of love, find a way to actively celebrate and confirm that love. Don't just develop the intention to give a gift to someone you love; actually present a real gift. If we lived in the world of space, then potentiality by itself would be fine. But we live in a material world, so we all need actualization. Consider reconnecting with people from your past who can benefit from your help or acknowledgment, especially people with whom you had a meaningful relationship. Call them, write them, thank them, remember them. Paint a picture, write a song, take a journey. To allow joy to manifest, you can buy a nice new outfit for yourself, or hang a nice thangka over your shrine.

   You allow the demons of anger, pride, or jealousy to manifest out in a nirmanakaya form—why not kindness and joy as well? To maintain the strength of manifestation beyond the meditation cushion, it is important to engage and give form to it. Have a specific date and plan in mind. Reconnect with the openness and clarity and then begin the action.

HEALING SOUNDS: CLEARING THE PATH OF THE CHANNELS THROUGH SOUND

You can find nearly any kind of medication in a home medicine cabinet—drugs to ease your pain, calm you down, send you into a deep sleep, and make you more alert. Suppose there was also a medicine that could awaken wisdom or that could restore continuity to awareness. This kind of healing potential is accessible in the form of healing sounds. A chapter of the Bön *Mother Tantra* entitled the "Commentary of Entering the Path of Method" describes various syllables you can sound to remove mental obscurations, cut through energy blocks, and even heal pain and physical illness.

How can sound heal a physical ailment? Every part of your physical body has a foundation of space, and in space there are awareness and energy. When these three aspects—open space, clear awareness, and spontaneous energy—are not in harmony, physical illness may form. It can be important to rely on conventional healing methods to treat the form of an illness, for example, having surgery to remove diseased tissue. But you can also focus on healing the space, awareness, and energy through the use of sound. Combined with the breath and prana, sound not only can help alleviate the symptoms of illness, it can also address the source of illness. Nothing is guaranteed, but a strong possibility for healing through sound exists.

These teachings are fascinating. They state clearly that sounding the syllable *HIK* helps to cure a headache, for example, and *HA PHU* helps to ease back or chest pain. This may seem like reciting a magical incantation, but it works. The practice of sound is similar to acupuncture, in which a needle placed in one area affects another location by enhancing the circulation of prana. The vibration of sound in one part of the body affects another area of the body, such as the liver or stomach. Not only can sound help you to overcome physical illnesses, but by clearing blockages in the chakras, it also helps you cultivate wisdom and thus aids your spiritual development.

Very few people are aware of the amazing healing potential of sound. Ancient yogis have relied on techniques such as these to maintain their health while living in remote areas far from medical care. I too have had a lot of positive experiences using many of these syllables, and so have my students. If you try these practices yourself and incorporate them into your life, the healing power of clear, pure sound will always be available whenever you need it.

Like Learning to Dance

The *Mother Tantra* tells us that learning how to apply healing sounds is like learning dance movements, Think of how certain dance movements send us leaping and others send us dipping or spinning. Similarly, some sounds have more of a releasing effect, others more of a contracting effect. Some retrieve, some expand, some guide, some give birth to certain energies.

It is not necessarily easy to understand all the dynamics related to how and why these syllables help in healing. As the teachings suggest, the best approach is to experiment and practice with each of the different methods so you can learn from your own experience how helpful and reliable they may be.

As with the primordial warrior syllables and other sound practices, the power of healing comes from your spiritual focus as you connect with the sound's physical vibration, its subtle energetic quality, and the space at the source of sound.

You can have good results when voicing these syllables strongly with lots of vibration, sounding them softly with little vibration, or reciting them without voice, using breath alone. The breath might be said to have more of a psychic than a physical level of vibration. The gross breath—the physical act of breathing out and in—carries the subtle breath known as prana, and prana is what carries the mind (see chapter 12, "Mind and Prana in Meditation Practice"). The prana is able to carry your consciousness into the body's organs and cells, as well as into your personal energy field. Both sound and breath can support you in realizing the connection between prana and mind.

Ten Sounds That Heal

Ten healing sounds are described below. When working with any of them, try reciting each syllable or pair of syllables twenty-one times, then repeat as needed. By practicing with just one sound over a period of time, you can get a better sense of how well it works for you.

It's good to sit up straight and keep the eyes open while reciting, but if visual distraction keeps you from connecting deeply with the sound, try practicing with your eyes closed. If you use a lot of breath when voicing certain syllables, be careful not to overdo it so as to avoid hyperventilation and dizziness.

▶ *PHET!* "cuts" the distorted mind. Sounding *PHET!* (*"pé!"*) cuts through the energetic aspect of your attachments at a very deep level. In sound practice this syllable is usually expressed as a strong burst of sound, like a rifle report. As the sound pierces, it shakes your entire experience of body, energy, breath, and mind.

We are very good at creating our own fears, emotions, mental projections, energy blocks, fixated thought patterns, and nightmares. Sounding *PHET!* is a way to deconstruct these creations, dissolving them back into space. This process is similar to when the wild lamas of Tibet would hit their students with a text to help them shift their patterns and gain realization. Any surprise can immediately cut through the patterns of body, energy, thoughts, and memories. The effect is like typing on a computer, using the "select" key to highlight the words you want to erase, and then, with "*PHET!*," pressing "delete."

Before sounding *PHET!* relax in your body. Take a few deep breaths. Try to be clear in your mind, and through that clear awareness bring into consciousness whatever obstacles, blocks, emotions, or other problems you are facing. For example, suppose you have just awakened from an intense nightmare about a car accident. Take ten to fifteen seconds to focus on the images of the crash, the energetic feelings of the experience, and all the effects on your body, prana, consciousness, and subconscious. Then you can bring a deep breath directly into this experience, and after concentrating it all together—like forming a snowball with your awareness right in the center—sound a strong *PHET!* Immediately, everything dissipates. When the experience is imagined as a snowball, not as something hard and insoluble, it can melt away into space. In place of the car crash image, there is now another image or no image at all. If the disturbing experience persists, you can repeat *PHET!* a few more times.

This syllable is particularly effective in cutting through energetic aspects of a problem. If there is a lot of conceptual meaning associated with your problem, try stepping back from it and seeing it as pure energy before inhaling and sounding *PHET!*

▶ **HA PHU eases pain and discomfort of the heart, lungs, chest, or back.** These two syllables (*"ha poo"*) have a releasing effect. They are recited in a single, long, drawn-out tone.

Before reciting them, draw attention to the location of your physical discomfort. The discomfort has a specific sensation, a sense of tension or resistance, and a very specific kind of energy, so try to connect with all these aspects. Not only are you recognizing the pain as an observer, but you are also feeling it as the one who experiences it.

Breathe in through the nostrils. As you do, imagine you are breathing prana right into the area of discomfort. Feel a slight movement and pressure in the muscles and tissues there, as if they are being massaged by the breath. Then, sound the syllables: *HAAA PHUUU.* As you release the sound and breath, feel that the entire experience with all its tension and resistance is being released through the prana. Also notice any effects of the sound's physical vibration in releasing and dissipating the pain and discomfort.

Most people are familiar only with breathing in the nose, lungs, and chest, so breathing directly into the back or heart may sound strange, but clearly it can be done. By visualizing in this way, you are focusing your practice directly on the area that needs healing, just as when you give a massage, you work only on the specific muscles that need loosening.

Saying *HA PHU* with more breath brings an increased sense of letting go. As you sound *PHU*, you can extend the release by blowing out through pursed lips. In addition, singing with a deeper tone and lower frequency can help you to connect more with an experience of yourself than with an experience of sound directed outward. A tone with more bass to it, it seems, is more connected to the base of all.

► *HIK* **cures a headache.** This syllable is sounded as a short burst of sound and works in a similar way to the syllables above. Focus on the location and feeling of the pain, its energetic quality, and any images, and so on. Breathe into the experience, then recite *HIK!* several times. Feel that as you expel the sound, breath, and prana, the pain and all associated experiences are being expelled and released, dissolving completely into space.

There is an alternative headache remedy mentioned in a separate text, which is simply to visualize while meditating that you have no head. People often laugh when I suggest this idea, but it works: the moment you feel the absence of your head, your headache is gone. We usually ascribe so much importance and concrete reality to our heads that our headaches can become just as real and important.

Our tendency to concretize our experience is a very serious matter, and according to the Bön Buddhist teachings, it is the first and most important error we make. The more concrete we make a problem, the greater it becomes. The more spacious and luminous our experience is, the less we will be affected by any of the challenges that meet us.

► *HUNG HRI* **calls the goddess to awaken calm abiding.** These two syllables (*"hoong hree"*) are normally sung in one long, drawn-out note. A good time to sound *HUNG HRI* is when you are feeling agitated or distracted. Sounding them helps you to connect with the goddess associated with them, who permits you to recognize and realize the deep sense of peace and calm that already exists within you. You can think of sounding *HUNG HRI* as the way to call the distant goddess to you and request her assistance. Or, you can imagine that she is already here within you and that sounding these syllables gradually dissipates all your anger, agitation, restlessness, or other emotional or energetic disturbances. When these disturbances are removed, you are brought in touch with the sense of calm and inner peace that is the goddess.

▶ *HUNG* **gathers or retrieves what has been dispersed.** Sound this syllable as one long, drawn-out note over and over if you are feeling scattered and need to develop concentration and focus. In this case *HUNG* is not manifesting a wisdom quality as in the Five-Warrior-Syllables Practice; here it brings concentration and focus.

▶ *OM HUNG* **brings continuity to interrupted awareness.** Said together as a long, drawn-out tone, these two syllables (*"ohm hoong"*) help to minimize mental distractions. For example, when you are abiding in a state of focused, blissful awareness during a meditation session and the positive experiences start to subside, you can sound *OM HUNG* to maintain continuity of focus. The syllables can be sounded when you are involved in any endeavor that requires continuous, focused awareness.

▶ *HE* **makes what is weak or wan more vivid.** In a good meditation session, the mind of the practitioner should be not only relaxed but also sharp, clear, and focused. Sounding *HE* (*"hé"*) in a long, drawn-out tone helps to sharpen and strengthen a weak or thin awareness.

The following three sounds also support higher experiences of the mind and help to overcome obstacles to meditation practice. Each is normally sung in a long, drawn-out tone:

▶ *HI HING* (*"hee hing"*) calls the master to awaken the knowledge within.

▶ *HU HUNG* (*"hoo hoong"*) causes the yidam to laugh in order to awaken the power and certainty within.[18]

▶ *A YANG* (*"ah yang"*) uplifts what has been diminished or degraded.

---

18. A yidam is an enlightened deity. Chapter 11, "Entering the Mandala," gives more information about yidams; see especially the section "The Meaning of the Mandala."

All ten of these healing sounds have been relied on by Tibetans since ancient times with good results. Often we may feel that we need a more complicated, analytical method of healing; if it's only one step— *PHET!*—then it couldn't possibly work. But in fact simple, direct trust in energetic healing through sound can have immediate, powerful effects. When it works, it doesn't take much time to demonstrate its effectiveness. If it doesn't work right away, then time is not likely to make a difference.

Working with healing sounds is initially a question of having trust, then gradually gaining some experience, and in the end having some realization. It is by working with the sounds that you can find out for yourself the value and authenticity of these teachings.

The *A Li Ka Li* Mantra

The ancient *A Li Ka Li* mantra incorporates all the Tibetan vowels and consonants. It is actually formed of two separate strings of mantra: *A–Li*, the vowels; and *Ka–Li*, the consonants. You can recite it in order to minimize impure speech and connect with your deeper self through pure sound. The Healing Practice of Chétak Ngomé (next in this chapter) combines the same alphabetic mantra with a more complex tantric visualization, enabling the practitioner to receive all the blessings and empowerments of enlightened speech.

To a Westerner, the *A Li Ka Li* mantra may look foreign and exotic, but in practice, it is solid and clear. In the monastery, people recite it very early in the morning, when the mind is clear and peaceful and thoughts are not completely activated. When I was growing up in India, we would get up early, collect dry wood for the fire, and then prepare breakfast. Throughout this routine, people would recite this mantra instead of conversing. They knew that saying all these syllables would have a specific effect on their health, mind, emotions, and practice, so they recited the mantra many times.

This mantra puts into action all of the "eight origins of sound," described in chapter 6. It's like chiropractic for the speech. The *A Li Ka Li* mantra exercises the lips, tongue, palate, and the other muscles used while talking and sharpens the speech. Even for people whose native language is not Tibetan, there is benefit from reciting these Tibetan syllables. I hear Westerners speak of the elemental tones that are missing in speech—for example, someone will have "no fire in their talk." Because of its complete system of vowels and consonants, this mantra provides a very balanced way of connecting with sound's different physical origins, vibrations, and elements, and it thus has real potential for purification and healing.

It's fine to say the mantra quickly, but not so quickly that clear pronunciation is lost. You can recite it while making your bed or while taking a shower. Instead of saying, "I can't talk until I've had my coffee," the mantra can be your morning cup of coffee. The whole idea is that this is a normal and beneficial practice to do each day.

The Mantra as Taught by Lishu Taring

Nyachen Lishu Taring was an eighth-century siddha, or accomplished master, who played a crucial role in the propagation of Bön in Tibet. He was a contemporary of the foremost Bön master Drenpa Namkha, who is said to be the father of the Buddhist saint Padmasambhava. At a time when Bön was threatened with eradication, Lishu Taring was known to have translated and concealed sacred texts for the benefit of future generations. Lishu Institute, a residential study center I recently founded in India, is named after him.

Around the eighth century, the prominent female master Choza Bemo requested a teaching from Lishu Taring. She asked, "How can I transform all my speech into mantra?" Lishu Taring responded with this teaching known as "The Supreme Recitation of A Li Ka Li: The Practices of Twelve Vowels and Thirty Letters" (*A–Li Décho*).

▸ **The morning practice.** At daybreak, "when the crow leaves the nest," visualize an eight-petaled red lotus on your tongue. On the petals visualize and feel the presence of sixteen seeds of *A–Li*, two syllables per petal:

A AH I II U UU RI RII LI LII E EE O OO ANG A

These syllables are pronounced as follows:

AH AHHH, EE EEEE, OO OOOO, RI REEEE, LI LEEEE,
Ā ĀĀĀĀ, OH OHHH, ANG AH

In the center of the lotus, visualize and feel the presence of your own sacred deity—the yidam or other deity to whom you feel a deep personal connection. Recite the following mantra of *A Li Ka Li* twenty-one times. As you recite, be aware of the eight different origins of sound (see chapter 6). They will all be simultaneously activated by the mantra.

A AH I II U UU RI RII LI LII E EE O OO ANG A
KA KHA GA GHA NGA
CHA CH'A JA JHA NYA
TA THA DA DHA NA
PA PHA BA BHA MA
TSA TS'A DZA DZ'A WA
ZHA ZA A YA
RA LA SHA SA
HA A
RA-KSHA RA-KSHA

If you begin your morning with this practice, throughout the remainder of the day, all of your speech—whether negative, neutral, or positive—will be more like a mantra.

▶ **The evening practice.** At dusk, "when the crow returns to the nest," visualize that the seed syllables on the petals dissolve into light and recite either the *Al Li Ka Li* or the *Ka Li* mantra (that is, all the lines above except for the first line of vowels) twenty-one times. When you do this, all the qualities of your speech will be pure in the evening.

THE HEALING PRACTICE OF CHÉTAK NGOMÉ: USING SOUND TO PURIFY AND EMPOWER YOUR SPEECH

The Healing Practice of Chétak Ngomé is a method for purifying and empowering your speech. Chétak Ngomé is a deity of speech whose practice is described in a teaching by Shardza Rinpoche, the master mentioned in chapter 3. This practice combines tantric visualization with the *A–Li* vowels and *Ka–Li* consonants. Through it you can receive all the blessings and empowerments of enlightened speech.

The Practice

Assume the five-point meditation posture, as described in chapter 4. Exhale the stale breath three times. Find the ground within yourself and rest. In clear space, transform instantly into the deity of speech, Chétak Ngomé, red in color. Feel your body become lighter, less substantial, more flowing, with a quality of vibration. In your right hand you hold a lotus whose petals are adorned with the *A–Li* seed syllables, the sound vibration of all the Tibetan vowels: *A AH I II U UU RI RII LI LII E EE O OO ANG A*

As Chétak Ngomé, draw attention to your heart. Within the heart is the red syllable *HRI*. From *HRI* red light emanates into infinite space, to the space of the enlightened beings where it retrieves the blessings and empowerment of the speech of all the deities and of all the sacred teachings, sounds and dharma texts. The light returns, reenters your body through the crown of your head, and dissolves into the red *HRI* in your heart. You become one with the light and thus receive the blessings and empowerment of the enlightened speech of all the buddhas.

On your tongue visualize a lotus of red light with eight petals. On the lotus are three rings of mantra, each spinning rapidly counterclockwise: at the center of the lotus is a mantra ring of the five warrior syllables:

A OM HUNG RAM DZA

Surrounding this inner ring is a mantra ring of the *A–Li* vowels:

A AH I II U UU RI RII LI LII E EE O OO ANG A

On the third, outer mantra ring are the *Ka–Li* consonants:

KA KHA GA GHA NGA CHA CH'A JA JHA NYA TA THA DA DHA NA PA PHA BA BHA MA TSA TS'A DZA DZ'A WA ZHA ZA A YA RA LA SHA SA HA A RA-KSHA RA-KSHA

As you continue to visualize and feel the three mantra rings spinning rapidly on your tongue, recite the *A Li Ka Li* mantra at least 7, 21, or 108 times:

> *A AH I II U UU RI RII LI LII E EE O OO ANG A*
> *KA KHA GA GHA NGA*
> *CHA CH'A JA JHA NYA*
> *TA THA DA DHA NA*
> *PA PHA BA BHA MA*
> *TSA TS'A DZA DZ'A WA*
> *ZHA ZA A YA*
> *RA LA SHA SA*
> *HA A*
> *RA-KSHA RA-KSHA*

As you recite, visualize that light from the *Ka–Li* mantra on the third, outer mantra ring goes up to the enlightened dimension and touches the enlightened speech of the deities and dharma texts. The light retrieves the blessings and empowerment of enlightened speech and returns to your own tongue where it dissolves into the *A–Li* mantra spinning on the second mantra ring. In this way you receive the blessings and empowerment of speech, and all the impurities, negative misdeeds and negative karmas of speech are purified.

Then light from the spinning *Ka–Li* mantra on your tongue goes out to all sentient beings, purifying and empowering their speech. The light returns and enters the *A–Li* mantra on your tongue. In this way you receive the empowerment of worldly speech qualities such as singing, speaking, writing, and composing poetry.

While continually reciting the mantra, feel a synchronized flow of light and blessings to and from all the enlightened beings and sentient beings. Feel a continuous sense of healing.

At the end of the recitation, continue to visualize the eight-petaled lotus of red light, feel the vibration of your tongue, and experience the connection to the speech of the enlightened dimension and to all sentient beings.

As the sound dissolves into silence, rest in the silence. Dedicate the merits of your practice to the enlightenment of all sentient beings.

Using Sound to Introduce You to the Nature of Mind: The Practice of Pure Inner Sound from Kündröl Dakpa

One might say that the practice of inner sound is the highest form of sound practice. It is based on a Bön dzogchen text entitled *Heart Drop of the Dakini* (Heart Essence of the Goddess), composed by the renowned master and scholar Kündröl Dakpa.

One reason this practice is seen as a very sacred teaching from the goddess is that it offers a direct introduction to the pure space of sound and the essence of your self. Done as a personal retreat in the absence of external sound, this unique dzogchen practice supports the experience of pure inner sound arising from the void. It is another example of a traditional method that enables you to hear sound, and listen to the listener, without interference from words, ideas, philosophies, or other concepts.

The Inner-Sound Retreat

The intensive personal retreat described below should be done only in a supportive setting with proper instruction and personal guidance from an authentic, experienced master because of the risk of psychological or other disturbances arising during practice as well as the potential for harboring an incorrect view. However, even if you don't plan to do the practice, it can be helpful to read through this section because it enhances the understanding of how to work with sound at its purest levels. At the end of this section, I have included instructions for a modified meditation practice that anyone can do to experience a glimpse of meditating with inner sound.

Traditionally, the practitioner will plan a full retreat alone in a very quiet, peaceful location. You can enter the retreat either during the day or night. A natural material such as clean, fresh cotton is used to close off the outer ear canal so that external sounds cannot enter and you will be able to hear the inner sound.

Begin by assuming the five-point meditation posture in order to keep the subtle channels open and thus set the conditions for the deeper experiences of inner sound. Next, maintain a vow to be still, silent, and spacious:

- ► Develop the strong intention to remain physically still.
- ► Vow to remain silent—like a person who has not been able to talk in many years and thus has let go of all intention to speak.
- ► Rest the mind in the space of pure awareness, trying not to follow thoughts of the past, plan the future, or change the present.

By maintaining these three vows, all you can do now is be, and so you will be able to hear and connect with the inner sound more clearly and directly.

While maintaining the five-point meditation posture, practice the *bumchen* (big vessel) breathing method. This is done by inhaling and holding your breath in the area four finger-widths below the navel. As you hold, compress the breath from both above and below by contracting gently upward with the muscles at the base of your pelvis while pushing down with the muscles of your diaphragm. Continue to hold the breath in this way, and focus on the inner sound.

Generally, it is good to begin with many short, clear meditation sessions and as the practice develops, engage in fewer, longer sessions as appropriate. Between sessions you should remain relaxed and quiet and just abide. You can recite mantras in your mind, but you should avoid engaging in internal dialogue that activates emotions or conceptual thoughts. More specific oral instructions on meditation technique and other practical considerations, including the best practice schedule to follow throughout the day, should be obtained from a qualified teacher.

Working with Experiences

According to Kündröl Dakpa's teaching, by following the above instructions the retreatant will begin to hear the inner sound within two to three days. By the fourth to fifth day, the experience of inner sound will become much stronger, even earsplitting and hard to tolerate. Then, after perhaps seven to eight days of practice, the inner sound will begin to taper off. After many days of practice, the sound may cease altogether.

As the retreat progresses, the practice of inner sound may be accompanied by strong experiences of dullness, agitation, or other obstacles to the practice. Kündröl Dakpa recommends remedies such as these:

> *If you experience weakness and lack of energy*, eat foods richer in protein.
>
> *If you become agitated*, massage the body with oil to address wind disorders (pranic disturbances). Take deep, calming breaths.
>
> *If the inner sound becomes too strong*, remove the cotton or other material from your ears while maintaining awareness. Once the inner sound becomes tolerable and you feel more relaxed, you can replace the cotton and continue with the practice.

If you feel fear as you draw closer to your center, it may drive you away from whatever experience arises. This is how fear works in our lives. At the moment fear arrives, be aware of it but not driven by it. Return your focus to the sound rather than engaging with the fear. Feel the fear, allow the fear, but continuously connect to the sound. That way you will maintain and deepen your awareness.

Auditory hallucinations may be another potentially unsettling effect of the practice. In normal life, "hearing voices" is often considered a symptom of mental illness. In the context of the inner sound practice, however, it is common to hear voices in the silence as the experience of inner sound intensifies. How do you incorporate this phenomenon into the practice of abiding in the nature of mind? Listen to the sound of the voice and be with it without rejecting it or trying to create more of it. Understand that no matter how wonderful or terrible it seems, the voice is only a self-arising manifestation. If you have a lot of anger, you may hear angry yells. If you tend to be fearful, you may hear many fearful sounds. If more enlightened qualities prevail, you may hear voices of the deities. Try not to apply much meaning to these sounds or to feel much attachment or aversion to them. Whatever form it takes, inner sound is your access to the internal space from which all sound self-manifests, which is the essence of your being.

Some people hear a constant phantom noise, commonly a ringing in the ears, as soon as they are exposed to even brief periods of silence. This may be a common condition called *tinnitus*, which is related to nerve damage. Although it has no external source, tinnitus is not what we call self-arising sound. Inner sound is a more subtle experience akin to inner thoughts and feelings—for example, to the experience you have when connecting deeply with the sound of chanting, prayers, or the beating of a ritual drum in a monastery. If you have tinnitus and it distracts you from the inner sound meditation, try practicing with the tinnitus itself. Like your own breath, the sound of tinnitus is close to you, and it can be another doorway to the inner silence. Try not to experience it as a problematic noise separate from you and instead connect with it as pure sound. By practicing in this way for long enough, through the sound you can connect to the source of the sound, which is your self, the base of all (*künzhi*), the mother.

Signs of Success

You can tell that the inner-sound practice is bearing fruit when you begin to experience the sound of sacred syllables arising from the inner voidness and moving through your body. In Tibet, practitioners have been known to engage in the inner-sound practice for a month or longer. Within that period of time, skillful practitioners may be able to achieve the result in which all sound, both internal and external, has less conceptual meaning. They discover a greater meaning in sound, and what they hear no longer affects them. They have exhausted their attachment to all those words and other external samsaric sounds that used to have solid meaning. They have discovered inner pure sound. In the end, the teachings say, the inner sound just stops. When it does, that moment is the discovery of one's self through silence.

Benefits of the Practice

Closing the ears and listening to the inner sound, being with it, connecting with it, brings you to a beautiful meditative experience of yourself that is very pure. Over time it helps you lose your attachment to beautiful sounds and your aversion to ugly sounds. You are no longer attached to hearing someone tell you how attractive you look—you already feel beautiful. You experience who you are, and who you are is complete. One cannot be more complete than who one is.

What you can gain with this practice applies not only to this lifetime. As described in chapter 3, "The Body of Light," shortly after death, after the elements dissolve and one's gross perceptions cease, one enters a kind of blank state. At some point the subtle winds come and with them the first arising of the three visions of sound, light, and rays. If you have practiced diligently and become familiar with your connection to the pure inner sound, hearing the sound arising in the bardo will help you to immediately recognize it as inner sound, and through that recognition you will be able to connect with the mother voidness and the son awareness. When the three visions are recognized as self-arising, not separate from your own self, you have the possibility to remain grounded in the natural state and achieve final liberation.

A Modified Inner-Sound Practice

Anyone can get a taste of practicing with inner sound in just one brief session by following these simple instructions:

Find a quiet place where you will not be disturbed.

Assume the five-point meditation posture.

Take three slow, deep breaths and relax. Bring your attention to your heart and let it rest there with open awareness.

Maintain the vows of stillness, silence, and spacious, thought-free awareness.

Use your fingers to press your ears tightly closed. This enables you to immediately experience the inner sound. Listen to it. Be with it. If the attention wanders, simply bring it back to the sound and maintain your awareness. Through the sound, connect with your center. This pure sound is coming from within and is completely neutral. You can either enter deeply into the place of the sound or feel that the sound itself is arising from that deep place, from your center.

Understand that you are not so much listening to inner sound as listening to the listener who is the source of the sound. You are being with künzhi, the mother, the source. If it seems as though you are listening to someone or something separate from you, change your approach and connect with the listener through the sound in a clear, pure way.

PART 3

Undeluded Mind
trulwa mépé thug

Introduction to Mind 9

Mind is clear and aware.
—TRADITIONAL DEFINITION IN TIBETAN BÖN BUDDHISM

The nature of the mind is the great clear light.
—PRAJÑAPARAMITA UPADESA BY ARYADEVA

JUST AS THE body has a clear and eternal aspect and speech a perfected and ceaseless aspect, so the nature of mind is radiant and
undeluded. Undeluded mind is always clear with the presence of light.
Clear refers to the empty, spacious, unchanging aspect of mind; light to
the mind's unceasing quality of self-awareness. The clear light of your
mind's nature has never been minimized or obscured by thoughts or
emotions. In every given moment, the doorway to this clear, luminous
mind is there for you. In the most confused moment, the most annoyed
moment, the most emotional moment, the door is always there. It is a
question only of knowing where the doorway is and entering it.

When speaking of mind as a doorway, it is important to understand
the distinction between *mind* and *nature of mind*. The mind we are
most familiar with is the "pain mind," the one busy with concepts,
thoughts, judgments, fantasies, emotions, and images. The conceptual
mind has a dualistic vision of our existence—it identifies as the subject
versus object, me versus not me, mine versus not mine. What it wants
and desires, it grasps at; what it fears or dislikes, it pushes away. It is
constantly comparing good with bad, right with wrong, important with
unimportant, attractive with unattractive.

Any thought can manifest in the mind. But when the mind stops thinking and instead turns inward and nakedly observes itself, observing the observer, mind liberates into its own nature like clouds dissolving into the sky or waves dissolving into the ocean.

The nature of mind is rigpa, pure nondual awareness. It is the absence of thought. It is neither virtuous nor nonvirtuous, substantial nor insubstantial. It has unlimited potential to manifest. Its essence is one with the essence of all that exists. Rigpa is sometimes likened to a mirror: just as reflections come and go without leaving the slightest trace on the mirror's surface, so do all experiences, memories, emotions, and mental images arise and dissolve in our mind without leaving a trace in the nature of mind.

When the nature of mind is unrecognized, it manifests as the moving mind. When known directly, it leads us to liberation. It *is* liberation. It is undeluded and radiant like a crystal—like the nirmanakaya, the movement of energy that arises from open awareness, the inseparability of emptiness and clarity.

No matter how confused or emotional the mind is, the mind's nature is always clear, pure, and undeluded. That is why entering the path to liberation is only a matter of our finding a doorway to what is already in us. If we have the right eye to see with, that is the doorway to wisdom. If we look with the wrong eye, we see only deluded objects and will not discover the undeluded mind.

There is a story that illustrates the opening of the eye that sees undeluded mind. Once there was a king who was captured and imprisoned by an enemy army. As a king, with all of a king's power, ego, and expectations, he had a lot to try to hold on to. But he was subjected to many weeks of torture—physical, emotional, and spiritual—and over time everything he identified with and embraced was taken from him by force.

One day the king was tortured in a public setting, and this wrenched away his pride and ego. By his next torture session, he had let go of some of his attachment to his ego but was still very fearful. By the next session, some of his fear was gone, yet his mind continued to grasp onto his physical body. In time his teeth were broken, his bones were broken, and he had no hair left on his head. Finally, one momentous day he looked up to see the faces of townspeople joining in on his torture, yet none of the faces was familiar to him—he had no connection with any of these people, had never done anything to hurt them. On seeing this, he could no longer even grasp the reason for all the abuse.

At that moment he had a deep realization: "Now they can do anything to me!" He had nothing to hold on to, there was nothing left to take. His mind completely let go of its grasping and connected with a deep sense of freedom. In this way, through the physical, mental, and emotional anguish of torture, he was able to achieve the bliss of undeluded mind.

As long as you keep grasping, you have something to protect. When you release what you have, there is no more need to protect. When there is no need to protect, there is a feeling of great freedom. Not only is joy omnipresent, it is also quite easy to access as long as you are open to it. Sometimes I tell my students in a simple, humorous way, "Close your eyes and just feel joyful." When they try to follow my instruction, do they feel joyful? Yes, they really do. By the power of their connection and trust in me, they allow themselves to let go and open their eyes to the joy that is already there within them.

CLEARING AWAY THE CLOUDS

If the unstained nature of mind is hard to fathom, you can think of your mind as being like the sky on an overcast day. Looking up, it seems as though the sky itself has been obscured by the clouds. But if you travel by jet high above the clouds, you will see that the sky is always a vast, clear, luminous blue. The sky has never once been obscured to itself—it only seemed to be obscured because of your relation with the clouds. In the same way, your mind only seems to be obscured because of your relation with your thoughts and emotions. If you can focus on the open luminosity of your mind rather than be continually interrupted by your emotions and thoughts, you can have this experience of clear light any time.

Everything is perfected in the clear-light nature of mind, dzogchen tells us—everything from experiences of duality and suffering to experiences of openness and enlightenment. There is unlimited potential for any level of experience to arise at any time. However, the reality is that we are more easily drawn toward the dark side than toward the light. Driven by karmic forces, our conceptual mind tends to engage more with the clouds—the conditions of suffering—than with the causes of happiness.

It's not that we don't want happiness, it is that our dualistic thoughts tend to create such a depth of separation: "This is good, that is bad"; "I want this, I don't want that"; "This is mine, that is yours." Every time life sends a problem our way, whether it's with finances, parking, or a relationship, our thinking gravitates toward the complicated. The more complicated our thoughts become, the more complicated and obscured our experience becomes. We grasp at what we desire, and we push away what we are averse to. The more we grasp and push away, the more we lose contact with the deep sense of connection we long for. We lose contact with our sense of self, with our soul. It is this loss of connection, not the inevitable problems we encounter, that makes us suffer so deeply.

Our minds tend to gravitate toward the complicated even though we have abundant opportunities to feel loving, joyful, and connected. Because we are conditioned, we always feel we need a reason to experience love or joy, and we always need a better reason: "I'll allow myself to feel joyful once I get a higher-paying job . . . once my children are grown . . . once I've retired and moved to Florida." Or, "I'll be able to love my partner if she loses weight . . . if he starts picking up after himself . . . if he stops criticizing me."

For some people, though, all that's needed is a cup of coffee or a sunny, breezy day to make them smile. If you think about it, you'll realize that love and joy need no reason at all. Love and joy are a state of mind. They exist innately in you. As we say in dzogchen, love and joy are perfected in the base, in our essence. But it is important for you to recognize this truth through experience rather than through conceptualizing.

This is true in meditation practice as well as in daily life. The days when you feel good, well, happy, and balanced are not the days to struggle with an unfamiliar, complicated meditation practice for purify-

PLATE 1. Five-point meditation posture

PLATE 2. Loosening the Knot to Overcome Desire

PLATE 3. Loosening the Knot to Overcome Desire

PLATE 4. Fluttering the Silk Tassel Skyward to Overcome Jealousy

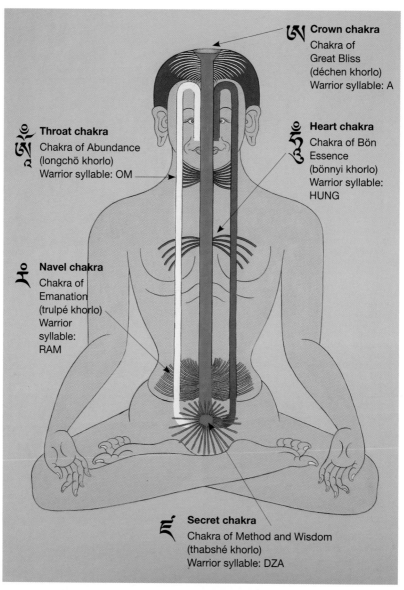

Crown chakra
Chakra of
Great Bliss
(déchen khorlo)
Warrior syllable: A

Throat chakra
Chakra of Abundance
(longchö khorlo)
Warrior syllable: OM

Heart chakra
Chakra of Bön
Essence
(bönnyi khorlo)
Warrior syllable:
HUNG

Navel chakra
Chakra of
Emanation
(trulpé khorlo)
Warrior
syllable:
RAM

Secret chakra
Chakra of Method and Wisdom
(thabshé khorlo)
Warrior syllable: DZA

PLATE 5. The three channels, five chakras, and five warrior seed syllables

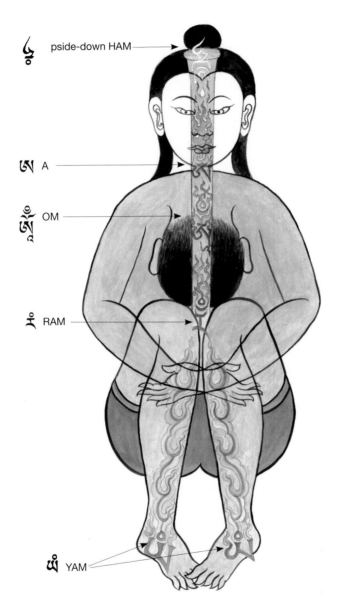

pside-down HAM

A

OM

RAM

YAM

PLATE 6. Visualization for the White Liquid Practice to Heal Disease

PLATE 7. *Ma Gyü* mandala (top view)

PLATE 8. (Below) Basic elements of the *Ma Gyü* mandala

Sangwé Yeshé
in union with Gawa Tsémé

Discriminating Wisdom

Red
West

Sangwé
Yungdrung
in union with
Tangnyom Tsémé

Wisdom of
Equanimity

Blue
South

Sangchö Gyelpo
in union with
Chéma Ötso

Wisdom of Emptiness

Yellow
Center

Sangwé Gyelpo
in union with
Champa Tsémé

All-
Accomplishing
Wisdom

Green
North

Rigpa Kuchuk in union
with Thugjé Tsémé

Mirrorlike Wisdom

White
East

PLATE 9. Yidam Sangchö Gyelpo and the four surrounding
yidams of the *Ma Gyü* mandala

PLATE 10. Shenlha Ökar, the divine being of light

PLATE 11. The Prostration

PLATE 12. The three root channels

PLATE 13. The life-force tsa lung exercise

PLATE 14. The life-force tsa lung exercise

ing your negative emotions. If you already have a quality of openness and love, your work is more to maintain that state. Meditate on it, familiarize yourself with it, cultivate it. Move with the wind of wisdom rather than against it. The days you are feeling angry or agitated can be the best times for purification practices or engaging more with physical movements and breathing exercises.

Meditation practices are like prescription medications: not every practice is good for every person in every situation. You need skill in choosing the right medicine to shift your mind's attention away from its clouds of confusion, anger, and suffering to a clear, joyful, centered experience of awareness, and then you need to cultivate that joyful experience. You also need a level of openness, faith, trust, knowledge, and experience.

The path to clear, luminous mind was originally taught by the Buddha. Bön Buddhism offers a wide variety of teachings and practices that make this original knowledge accessible to the practitioner, some of which are shared in these pages. As you read on, you may experience that this section on the door of the mind is not as clear-cut as the sections on body and speech. After all, it is relatively easy to separate out what is physical and what is energetic- or speech-based; but in the end everything is mind. Body, speech, and mind are inseparable. What this section does is explore wisdom teachings that clarify fundamental concepts particularly related to mind. For example, chapter 10 gives step-by-step instructions for realizing mind's empty nature as a direct pathway to experiences of union and bliss—serving equally as a teaching and a guided meditation. Chapter 11 reveals the tantric mandala as a doorway to the sense of wholeness and completeness that we are all seeking. Chapter 12 looks at mind's relationship to prana, and chapter 13 gives insight into how you can transform your entire universe by transforming the ego-based identity. This section on mind concludes with chapter 14, which consists of a series of related mind-based practices. For those interested, the exploration of mind continues in appendix 4, where I share some thoughts regarding the dual roles of Buddhism and science in achieving a happy, healthy mind.

STARTING FROM A CLEAR PLACE

Mind itself is not the problem. Mind is always clear and luminous. The sky is always clear and blue. Again, the question is one of finding and entering the doorway. All of the teachings in this book, in the end, are about accessing that doorway to the clear, luminous mind.

The teachings of dzogchen are considered particularly special because their knowledge enables one to connect in a direct and immediate way with this clear, aware mind that is the source of all. The dzogchen practices rely on only minimum engagement with the conceptual mind and its thoughts, whereas many other systems of Buddhism rely a great deal on theory and analysis.

Every problem we have is created by fear, hope, and our conditioned identity. But in our essence, none of these problems exists. If you engage too much with the conditioned aspect, you solidify, strengthen, and stabilize all the concepts and ideas surrounding it. When they are so familiar, they always arise. When they are so strong, they always stay a long time. When they are so real, we don't find any reason to prove they are not.

When a dzogchen practitioner confronts a problem in meditation, rather than investigating the interplay of all the conditional aspects associated with the problem, he or she observes *who* is creating the problem. Suppose, for example, that during meditation you call up the emotion of anger. If you focus primarily on the person who is the object of your anger, you are likely to have an experience of deluded mind. If you observe the emotion itself, you will experience less delusion. But if you look at *who* is angry and deluded, you immediately have no delusion. Delusion is self-liberated when you directly, nakedly, internally observe the observer. You discover pure wisdom right there, at the source of anger. In this way deluded anger becomes the door to discovering undeluded mind.

RIGHT MIND, WRONG MIND

Historically, there has been much debate between different Buddhist schools and within dzogchen itself about what sets dzogchen apart. The discussion always seems to come back to the same question: *Which mind understands the mind's nature?* If mind is always clear and luminous and if the door is always there, then what is the problem? Why don't we "get it"? Most likely, in our search for clear mind, we are always searching with the wrong mind.

A few years ago I completed a book in collaboration with Anne Klein that devotes its pages primarily to exploring this question, albeit from a generally philosophical perspective. Entitled *Unbounded Wholeness: Bon, Dzogchen, and the Logic of the Nonconceptual*, the book is a study and translation of *The Authenticity of Open Awareness*, a foundational text of the Bön Dzogchen tradition. As its introduction points out:

> The view established through reasoning is not the authentic state of open awareness. . . . Establishing the view is not a method for realizing the view. This significantly distinguishes the dzogchen presentation from, for example, Geluk's Madhyamika interpretations of Dignaga and Dharmakirti, where conceptual knowledge of the view is indeed an important step toward realization of it. . . . Conceptual knowledge does not lead to realization. . . . Open awareness cannot validly or authentically be known conceptually. In fact, this is the first helpful clue about what open awareness, or the unbounded wholeness it recognizes as itself, might be.[19]

When your view has any kind of boundary or filter, every experience you have will be colored by those limitations. For example, if you have a strong materialistic perspective, no matter how you look at things, you will always see them through the filter of materialism. It will be almost impossible to view things other than in relation to your children, your husband, your wife, your bank balance, the evening news, the weather, or other worldly issues. Similarly, an astronomer's

19. Anne Carolyn Klein and Geshe Tenzin Wangyal Rinpoche, *Unbounded Wholeness: Bon, Dzogchen, and the Logic of the Nonconceptual* (New York: Oxford University Press, 2006), 6–7.

observations of the universe will always be colored and defined by the limitations of his telescope lens and in which direction he happens to point it.

Many practitioners have a mistaken understanding of essential truths portrayed in the teachings since they view them only from the grasping mind. Not only their emotions, but also the antidotes—the enlightened qualities of love or joy, for example—are experienced based on the grasping mind. In a way this is how it must be since students can begin only from where they are. But trying to enter the nature of mind from the viewpoint of the grasping mind is like trying to pass through an airport security gate carrying a weapon: virtually every time you will fail to enter. When it comes to truly understanding the nature of mind and connecting with one's true self, one has to go beyond the grasping mind.

DOORWAYS TO RIGPA

Rigpa, or innate awareness, is valid direct perception: the nature that sees itself. According to *Unbounded Wholeness*, "[Rigpa] alone is fully aware of its own nature as unbounded wholeness. Its authenticity, we will finally be told, is an authenticity innate to reality; not, as with inference, an authentication *of* such reality."[20] Rigpa is beyond subject and object, beyond all duality. Only the state of rigpa can directly experience itself. The idea that one can't experience rigpa unless one experiences rigpa may seem like the ultimate catch-22. But luckily there are many doorways through which one can enter. Through the activity of the mind in meditation practice, we can realize the nature of mind.

Some of the practices in part 3 work with the breath, some with sacred seed syllables, and some—like the teaching by Dawa Gyeltsen described in the next pages—work directly with the mind itself. Through these practices, we can arrive at an experience where we can merge with inner space, with unconditioned self-realization.

20. Ibid., 8.

The Fivefold Teachings of Dawa Gyeltsen 10

Vision is mind
Mind is empty
Emptiness is clear light
Clear light is union
Union is great bliss

THESE FIVE LINES are the essence of a heart teaching by Dawa Gyeltsen, an eighth-century Bön meditation master. Dawa Gyeltsen was the twenty-fourth of a famous, unbroken lineage of masters of the dzogchen teachings of the *Zhang Zhung Nyen Gyü*, and his teaching is from a cycle of oral transmission of the Great Perfection known as *Nyam Gyü Dzogchen Kyamug*.

Like *Authenticity of Open Awareness*, Dawa Gyeltsen's fivefold teaching helps to guide the mind toward the authentic experience of rigpa. Yet his instructions are less an exercise in intellectual discourse and more a doorway to actual experience. Reflecting on each of these five simple lines in succession can guide you directly to the essence, to the root of your self, to the clear and blissful experience that is the nature of mind.

In applying the fivefold teachings as a practice of the mind, you aim to recognize each of the five principles one after another.

VISION IS MIND

How do we follow Dawa Gyeltsen's advice, which begins: "*vision is mind*"? Vision includes everything we perceive, but as an entrance to this exercise, I suggest you call up a vision that bothers you. You might begin with your "famous person," also known as your "karmic friend" or "karmic guest"—the one person who seems as though he or she was put on this earth to create problems for you. Most of us have a famous person in our lives.

While sitting in meditation, invite this person into your awareness. Look deeply at your experience: what exactly is this famous person composed of? Look directly at the person's character, at his or her energetic or emotional presence. Consider that at the time this person was born, he or she did not appear as you see him or her now. Also, consider that many other people know this person but do not share the same view you have of him or her. In fact, your own sense of identity is what has created this specific image.

In this moment, instead of focusing on the image as a substantial entity that is clearly separate from you and outside you, close your eyes, step back into yourself, and let the mental image come in. Reflect on the image and your experience.

This image is your vision. It is very much in you, in your mind. Perhaps you tend to feel self-protective, contracted, or agitated in the presence of this famous person. Feel this fully, not simply with your intellect. Sit with the image of your famous person and the resulting feelings and sensations until you recognize that this experience is in you, and conclude, "Vision is mind."

Mind Is Empty

The next question is: what is this mind? Look at your mind. Look from the top of your head to the soles of your feet. Can you find anything solid? Can you find any permanent color, shape, or form that you can call your mind? If you look directly, you come to the conclusion that *mind is empty.* Some people reach this conclusion very quickly; others need to undertake an exhaustive search to discover this spontaneous awareness. But this is what mind is. Your clarity of understanding may become polluted in any given moment, but by continuing to observe directly, you can discover that mind itself is just clear and open. What began as the gross reality of your famous person is now clear and open. If this is not your experience, you are still grasping the image and your experience in some way. Just be. Relax into the experience. No matter what vision appears, it is always empty. Just as waves in the ocean always have the nature of water no matter how peaceful or violent they may appear, vision always has the nature of emptiness. The essence is always there. When you arrive at the experience of emptiness and vastness through the doorway of the famous person, it is possible to have quite a strong experience of emptiness.

EMPTINESS IS CLEAR LIGHT

Now we can ask ourselves: what is this emptiness? It can be scary to confront the nothingness that is the absence of self, to the point that some people may prefer their famous person to emptiness. But the experience of open space is essential since in order to clear the obstacle you have to clear the identity that creates the obstacle. There is an expression, "The sword of wisdom cuts both ways." That is, the wisdom of emptiness cuts not only what is perceived but also the perceiver. Try not to be frightened by emptiness. Instead, remember that *emptiness is clear light*. It has light—the light of self-awareness. It is possible to feel this light in the absence of phenomena.

We tend to accumulate a lot of "stuff" in life: cars, furniture, appliances, books, knick-knacks, pets, and friends. We also collect opinions, emotions, and experiences. Every now and then we have a big yard sale to get rid of our old stuff. When we do, we may feel a certain lightness and relief at being free of it all. But very soon we become excited about all the new stuff we can accumulate to redecorate and fill the space that has opened up. In your meditation, when things clear, try to just be in the openness. Don't focus on the absence of the stuff but discover the presence of the light in that space. The light is there.

I'm not saying it's easy to recognize and connect with the light; your facility will depend on how caught up you are with appearances, including the image of your famous person. If you have more flexibility, when you look at the famous person and discover it is mind and then discover that mind is empty, the moment you see the space, you begin to clearly see the presence of clear light.

When you look for mind and don't find anything, the dzogchen instruction is to "abide without distraction in that which has not been elaborated." What has not been elaborated is that space, that openness. Abide there. Don't do anything, don't change anything, just allow. When you abide in that vast space without changing anything, your awareness of the emptiness is clear light. "Clear" refers to mind's empty, spacious aspect, and "light" refers to its quality of self-awareness, or clarity.

The only reason you have a famous person is that you see yourself as disconnected from the clear experience of the vast, open space. Not recognizing the vast space, not being familiar with it, you experience visions. Not recognizing the visions as mind, you see them as solid and separate and "out there"—and not only out there, but as disturbances that create hassles for you.

One can say, "I have clarity about my direction in life." Here, in emptiness, there is clarity as well, but it is not "clarity about something"; it is clarity in the sense of being. There is a clear experience of your essence, your existence, your being. That is the best kind of clarity. Through experiencing that clarity you overcome self-doubt.

CLEAR LIGHT IS UNION

Within this experience of vast emptiness, we now say to ourselves: *clear light is union*. Eastern spiritual traditions have many examples of two elements in inseparable union: yin and yang, male and female, wisdom and compassion, emptiness and clarity. If you try to look for clarity, you cannot find it—it becomes emptiness. If you abide in the emptiness, the emptiness becomes clarity. Clear light is union in the sense that these two are not separate. Clarity is simply the experience of emptiness. One cannot experience clarity without experiencing emptiness, and one cannot experience emptiness without experiencing clarity. These two are inseparable. Recognizing this is called union.

Because they are inseparable, no experience should have to affect our ability to remain open. Yet our experiences normally do affect our connection to openness because as soon as we encounter them, we become excited and attached or agitated, conflicted, or disturbed. When openness is unaffected by vision, when our experience spontaneously arises and does not obscure us, that is union: the inseparable quality of *clear* and *light*. We are free, we are connected. We are connected, we are free.

This combination is rare, whether in deep meditation or in everyday life. Often, if you are free, it means you are disconnected. If you say you'll be free on Tuesday, that probably means you won't be working that day—you'll be disconnected from work. If you are working, then you are not free, you are stuck. The sense of union, the ability to see things, do things, and be with people while still feeling open and free is very important. That is what is meant by "clear light is union."

UNION IS GREAT BLISS

If you recognize and experience this inseparable quality, then you can experience bliss. *Union is great bliss.* Why is there bliss? Because now you are released from that apparently solid obstacle or block that kept you from being deeply connected with your self. A strong experience of bliss spontaneously arises because nothing obscures you or separates you from your essence. You feel everything is complete just as it is.

You begin with the famous person and end with great bliss. What more could you ask for? This is the basis of the entire dzogchen view in five short lines. The entire process can be experienced in an instant—the moment you see your famous person, you can feel bliss. But sometimes we have to go through all the progressive stages. You must first understand the famous person as a vision, the vision as your mind, and that mind as empty. From there, emptiness is realized as clear light, clear light as union, and union as great bliss. Reaching this conclusion can take time.

One should also receive direct introduction to the nature of mind by a knowledgeable, experienced dzogchen master to ensure one does not practice with a mistaken view. But the fivefold instructions by Dawa Gyeltsen offer a clear map.

These five principles are a doorway to the nature of mind when applied as a formal daily practice, but they can also be recalled during difficult circumstances. You can remind yourself of them in any situation, in any given moment, and especially when the famous person is bothering you. Of course, when problems arise, there are likely to be many conventional solutions. But through this practice, there is the potential for more profound and lasting results.

At the beginning of a formal practice session, start by trusting with your heart and praying for a deep experience and the blessings of effortlessness. Perhaps you are feeling bad because you just lost a business deal; now, look at that sense of loss—it is a vision. Whether your vision is loss based, fear based, or greed based, you can look directly at your experience and be with that experience. You can realize that your vision is mind; then look at mind and discover that mind is empty. Even when you have a lot of problems, the essence of mind is always empty and clear. There is always the potential to connect with the essence of mind rather than with its confusion aspect.

I encourage you to follow this heart advice of Dawa Gyeltsen, to look directly into what is disturbing you and discover the nature of your mind. As you repeat this practice, the image of your famous person will not disturb you as much. Not only can you heal your day-to-day life and make it lighter and more pleasant, but through the profound simplicity of these five lines you can also recognize and connect with your innermost essence, the nature of your mind as Buddha.

Entering the Mandala: *The Psychological Dimension of the Mandala of the* Ma Gyü   11

I F YOU WATCH Tibetan monks creating a sand mandala, you can see in the brightly colored grains of sand an elaborate depiction of concentric geometric forms and intricate images. Whether a tantric mandala is drawn, painted, created from sand, or visualized by the mind in meditation, its purpose is to help the student become familiar and connect with a particular tantra and its central deity. Through entering the mandala, the student is able to enter directly into the mind or state of being of that deity.

The mandala encompasses the entire universe as well as a complete cycle of teachings and practices to achieve enlightenment. All the elements of the cycle of the *Ma Gyü* (Bön *Mother Tantra*)—all of the practices and thangka images, all of the wisdom teachings I have been giving Western students in the past decade about dream and sleep yoga, chö, elements, bardo, powa—are intimately related and are embodied in the mandala of the *Ma Gyü*.

People often have a notion of a mandala as representing a high, secret teaching: they love it because it's so elevated, but they don't have a sense of what it really means for themselves, their practice, and their lives. Distilled into its most essential elements, the structure of the *Ma Gyü* mandala is very clear. It is the doorway to the center of wholeness, to the center of one's being.

IN SEARCH OF WHOLENESS

When we think of what it means to be psychologically healthy, we imagine a sense of wholeness, of completeness—what psychiatrist Carl

Jung referred to as "individuation." Nothing is lacking. We feel open, free, and unencumbered. On the other hand, we all know what it is like to suffer emotionally and mentally. We continually feel as though something is wrong, as though something essential to our happiness and well-being is missing. We usually blame our unhappiness on external conditions such as an unsatisfying career, too much financial debt, disrespect from a loved one, or an illness that won't go away. As soon as we land a new job or our loved one apologizes, we may feel like everything in the world is right again. But that feeling of satisfaction is fleeting. Even if we win the lottery, new difficulties will arise sooner or later, and our grasping mind will always find new reasons to feel dissatisfied.

But what is it that really makes us suffer? It's not so much what is going on externally in our life but more that we are feeling blocked and our grasping mind is holding on to those blockages. It is our lack of openness that makes us feel incomplete.

What can end the cycle of suffering? The bottom line is, the more openness we are able to develop—whether physically, energetically, emotionally, conceptually, or psychically—the better and more complete we will feel no matter what difficulties arise. In particular, we need an enhanced quality of open awareness. This awareness is not the kind that is "aware of" something; it is without object and is unconditional. Open awareness is the key to cultivating wisdom. The very definition of rigpa, our true nature, is awareness of openness. All of the methods people use for self-actualization, such as psychotherapy, yoga, and dream work, are different ways to overcome fear, strengthen hope, and generate the open awareness that brings a greater realization of oneself. The *Ma Gyü* mandala, too, offers valuable insight into gaining the sense of wholeness we are seeking.

THE MEANING OF THE MANDALA

The teachings of the *Ma Gyü* are the seventh of nine vehicles in the Bön tradition, "the vehicle of white *A*," *A Kar Thegpa*. Figure 11.1 depicts a top view of the *Ma Gyü* mandala, while figure 11.2 depicts the deities inhabiting the mandala. Every aspect of these images has symbolic meaning, but what is most important about the deities is not what color they are; how many arms, legs, or faces they have; what they are wearing; or what ritual item they hold in their right hand: it is the essential meaning they portray.

▸ *The central yidam.* At the center of the *Ma Gyü* mandala—and at the core of our very self—is the main yidam Sangchö Gyelpo (King of the Supreme Secret), who is the embodiment of open awareness. As with every yidam in the Tibetan traditions, Sangchö Gyelpo is actually two enlightened beings in perpetual union: a male wisdom deity (Sangchö Gyelpo, the embodiment of pure space and openness) and his compassionate female consort, or *khandro* (Chéma Ötso, who embodies pure awareness and light).

▸ *The four surrounding yidams.* Surrounding the yidam Sangchö Gyelpo are four other yidams, each of which is associated with one of the four enlightened qualities of love, compassion, joy, and equanimity. Known as the "four immeasurables," these qualities are encompassed in a prayer often recited in the monastery:

> May all sentient beings enjoy happiness and the cause
>   of happiness.
> May all sentient beings be free from suffering and the cause
>   of suffering.
> May all sentient beings not be separated from the great
>   happiness devoid of suffering.
> May all sentient beings dwell in the great equanimity free
>   from [the bias of] suffering or happiness.

According to the teachings, *loving-kindness* (Tib. *champa*) is the mind that yearns for any and all beings to have happiness and its causes. *Compassion* (Tib. *nyingjé*) is the heartfelt wish that all beings may be free from suffering and its causes. Joy, or in this case *empathetic joy* (Tib. *gawa*), involves rejoicing in others' happiness and in their virtuous actions that are the cause of their future happiness. And *equanimity* (Tib. *tangnyom*) is an enlightened view that is not bound by dualistic thinking and is therefore beyond suffering and happiness. A broader definition of the four immeasurables can also incorporate our more conventional sense of love, compassion, joy, and equanimity.

In the mandala, the position of these four enlightened qualities around a center of open awareness reveals some fundamental truths. For one, the experience of inseparable space and light, or open awareness, is central to the experience of love, joy, equanimity, and compassion. Second, each of these four immeasurables in itself can serve as an entryway to the experience of open awareness and completeness. The mandala, essentially, is showing us two primary ways toward realization.

▶ **If we connect with undeluded mind, the immeasurable qualities will naturally arise.** When we are able to connect with the space and light of the central yidam, all the perfected wisdom qualities can spontaneously manifest. Not only does the inseparable state of open awareness give birth to love, joy, equanimity, and compassion, in a more profound sense it also gives birth to the entire mandala, to everything in the universe, to every infinite experience we have in our mind.

When awareness is open and clear, the light of love naturally radiates. Conventional love is based on our sense of identity or other conditions, such as a mother's love for her son or a citizen's love for his or her country. But when you connect with the center, unconditional love penetrates simply because wisdom and awareness penetrate and because the causes of hate—doubt, fear, and insecurity—are no longer hosted. We experience unconditional love the moment we discover the wisdom in ourselves.

Joy also naturally manifests from the blissful union of awareness and openness. We might think of the happiness of buying the car we've always wanted or of leaving the job we've always hated. But the unconditional joy that arises from openness is not the joy of having or owning. It is the simple joy of being.

Compassion also spontaneously manifests because open awareness leaves us no choice but to feel another's suffering as if it were our own. Many of us will feel empathy only if the object of our compassion appears deserving—for example, if the person seems sick or hungry enough and hasn't been doing anything to annoy us. Or, sometimes we will help someone because it seems like the right thing to do or because we know other people will notice our good deed. But the compassion that arises from inseparable space and light is not based on any such conditions.

Equanimity has to do with balance. When one is balanced in space rather than in forms or appearances, that is absolute balance. Feeling balanced in forms or appearances is actually a precarious state. If you told Sangchö Gyelpo, "I have equanimity because I have a secure job and a secure home," he would laugh for a week. At any moment, the places, things, people, and situations that support us can be destroyed. Think of the World Trade Center—within a few short hours, the twin towers became space. Many Tibetans in my parents' generation who escaped to India after the Chinese invasion of Tibet lost everything they owned, from the material to the spiritual. They came to a country where they didn't know the language and couldn't relate with the food or climate. Even highly respected teachers had to work on road construction. Inner equanimity is the most important equanimity.

Our external conditions are not the source of unconditional love, joy, compassion, or equanimity. The inseparable open awareness, the essence, is what gives birth to these four immeasurable qualities.

How do we develop this open awareness? Ultimately, the purpose of all the teachings and practices of the *Ma Gyü* is to help us connect with the inseparable space and light at the center of the mandala. Meditation practice requires some effort and approaching the center is not always comfortable. We can enter into deep meditation, have our first glimpse of the vast spaciousness, and fear immediately arises—the fear that this profound emptiness signifies the end of everything. When openness is vast but is clouded by doubt, there can be a lot of fear. But the truth is, when we are able to connect fully with the emptiness, with doubtless clarity, all of life begins from there.

Imagine transforming completely into the yidam Sangchö Gyelpo. You are the king of the supreme secret. At that moment, there is no

more secret; you know who you are. And you have four manifestations, each with a beautiful consort: love, compassion, joy, and
equanimity.

► **If we cultivate one of the four immeasurable qualities, we will experience a glimpse of the source.** An experience so simple and pure as
open awareness can be very difficult to connect with. Therefore, an
alternative route to the center of the mandala is to cultivate one or
more of the immeasurable qualities. When you develop a closer relation with one of the four deities who embody joy, love, equanimity,
and compassion, in a sense you can discover in that deity the essence,
Sangchö Gyelpo, and spontaneously realize the clear space and pure
light.

Which of the four gates do you open first? Try one that is easier
to enter, that is more accessible to you. Perhaps you are more familiar with the quality of love or perhaps you have experienced so
much suffering yourself that you can readily generate compassion
for others. Another way to choose the door is to first notice the emotions that may be causing you to disconnect from yourself. When you
can identify a disturbing emotion, you can determine the wisdom
quality that will help to counteract it and allow you to reconnect
with your self and your sense of completeness. For example, if you
are attached to feeling sad, disappointed, or unworthy, joy may be
the most direct antidote to those emotional blockages.

You can connect with and internalize the four immeasurables
by doing specific meditation practices such as the Five-Warrior-
Syllables Practice (see chapter 8) or simply by cultivating them in
daily life. For example, to cultivate joy, I can regularly remind myself
about how blessed my life is with a nice partner, good health, and
material possessions; whatever I have I can recognize as a gift and
feel joyful about it. The more I can feel that joy and cultivate it, the
more subtle and pervasive the quality of joy will become in my life.
One day it will be less dependent on what I have than on who I am.
My car may break down, and I may end up penniless, but I will
still feel the joy deep within me. That joy can carry me into being a
whole person.

From a deeper perspective, the good feelings and sense of wholeness arise when one feels unblocked, free and open. Joy is the flower of that openness. It is the color of it, the melody of it. Deep inside joy, the light is there, the space is there.

Just as the sound "ah" is the soul of every consonant in the Tibetan alphabet, space is at the base of every form, and awareness is within every experience of mind, in the same way, the essence is in every experience of open joy, love, compassion, and equanimity. Each of these four immeasurable qualities is important toward experiencing a greater sense of wholeness.

THE FIVE WISDOMS

Each of the five central deities of the mandala can also be an entryway to one of the very subtle levels of awareness known in the Bön Buddhist teachings as the five wisdoms:

▸ **The wisdom of emptiness** (associated with Sangchö Gyelpo) is the wisdom that realizes all phenomena lack inherent existence. Just as a magician knows all the trickery behind his magic act, the wisdom of emptiness recognizes the empty, illusory nature of all experience.

▸ **Discriminating wisdom** (associated with the consort known as the Goddess of Immeasurable Joy) is the wisdom that realizes every phenomenon as being clear and distinct in itself. Despite its empty nature even the subtlest experience of mind is seen as clear and distinct, with no intermingling. On a conventional level, we can think of a court judge as needing some discriminating wisdom. A judge must always maintain openness and impartiality yet at the same time must have the highest degree of clarity on all the fine points of law and must see precisely how each point stands on its own.

▸ **All-accomplishing wisdom** (associated with the Goddess of Immeasurable Love) is the wisdom that realizes all phenomena are spontaneously, effortlessly, and naturally perfected in the base of self-arising wisdom. The experience of all-accomplishing wisdom is one of completion—imagine how you would feel right after winning the mega-million dollar lottery, when you are no longer searching and striving because you have finally and completely arrived. When we lack this wisdom, we continually search outside ourselves for a sense of completion; we think the love or joy we want is "out there" somewhere and that we must struggle to find it. But if we realize love and joy are already in us, spontaneously perfected in our empty nature, then the all-accomplishing wisdom is there.

▶ **Mirrorlike wisdom** (associated with the Goddess of Immeasurable Compassion) is the wisdom that recognizes the clear, unobscured, and unchanging reflective quality of the base. When mirrorlike wisdom is lacking, the subject is affected by the object. The doctor is affected by his patients. The employee is affected by his job. The practitioner's meditative state is affected by his thoughts and emotions. When we connect with this wisdom, all phenomena are experienced as abiding in the base of self-arising wisdom like images reflected in a crystal-clear mirror. Like a mirror, the mirrorlike wisdom does not judge or grasp anything reflected in it: all visions self-arise, self-abide, and self-liberate without a trace.

▶ **The wisdom of equanimity** (associated with the Goddess of Immeasurable Equanimity) is the wisdom that realizes form and space are in equipoise. There can be no form without space; there can be no space without form. Every phenomenon in its place is in balance with space and inseparable from space. It is beyond good or bad, beautiful or ugly. For example, you might experience a taste of the wisdom of equanimity right after passing a final exam. Before the exam, you agonized about forgetting some of the answers; but now that you know you have passed, forgetting makes no difference. It is empty of meaning and importance. You now feel totally balanced in the experience of forgetting.

One of these wisdoms sees the aspect of space (openness); one sees clarity; one sees spontaneous perfection; one sees nongrasping awareness; one experiences a balance of clarity and emptiness. Just as the fivefold teachings of Dawa Gyeltsen present the truth to us in stages—vision is mind, mind is empty, emptiness is clear light, clear light is union, union is great bliss—these five wisdoms too can be viewed as stages of realization. Stages are useful in realizing the truth, but actually there are no stages and no separations. All five wisdoms ultimately are describing a single wisdom, the wisdom embodied by the central figure of the mandala, Sangchö Gyelpo in union with Chéma Ötso.

Who, then, is Sangchö Gyelpo, the king of the supreme secret? Obviously, the king of the supreme secret is oneself. You are the truth. You are Sangchö Gyelpo. He is called the supreme secret because not everyone has realized this truth; and he is called the king because by realizing one's self, one attains the center of power.

What the mandala is really telling us is that we are not separate from divine, enlightened beings. They are within us. The infinite experience of the human mind is based on the pure space in oneself. If we connect with that space, we connect with wisdom. All of our disturbing emotions are liberated instantly and have no power to be there, and the conditions that previously disturbed us become ornaments, enhancing our inner qualities and our being.

The mandala is the model through which a person can gain a clear understanding of wholeness. In turn, through understanding wholeness, one can come to understand the real meaning of the mandala and its images and the real meaning of the entire cycle of *Ma Gyü* teachings.

THE CENTRAL FIGURES

The five primary deities of the mandala of the *Ma Gyü* are:

▶ **The Yidam Sangchö Gyelpo.** The male figure Sangchö Gyelpo, blue in color, represents clear space or openness; his consort Chéma Ötso, red in color, represents pure light or awareness. Embraced in blissful union, these two figures represent the inseparable union of space and light; together they are referred to as one entity: the yidam Sangchö Gyelpo (Déchen Thodral, boundless great bliss). Sangchö Gyelpo is associated with the wisdom of emptiness and is trampling on the Demon of Ignorance.

▶ **The four surrounding yidams.** Surrounding the central yidam are his

Figure 11.1 *Ma Gyü* mandala (top view) (see also plate 7)

four manifestations, each a male deity in union with a goddess who represents one of the four immeasurables of joy, love, equanimity, and compassion.

▸ To the west is Sangwé Yeshé or Secret Primordial Wisdom, who is turquoise in color and in union with Gawa Tsémé, Goddess of Immeasurable Joy, red in color. This yidam represents discriminating wisdom and is trampling on the Demon of the Affliction of the Cycle of Attachment, or Demon of Sickness.

▸ To the north is Sangwé Gyelpo, or Secret King, who is blue in color and in union with Champa Tsémé, Goddess of Immeasurable Love, yellow in color. This yidam represents all-accomplish-

Figure 11.2 Yidam Sangchö Gyelpo and the four surrounding yidams
of the *Ma Gyü* mandala (see also plate 9)

ing wisdom and is trampling on the Demon of the Aggregates of
Becoming a Body, or the Demon of Aging.

▸ To the east is Rigpa Kuchuk, or Innate Awareness of the Cuckoo,
who is blue in color and in union with Thugjé Tsémé, Goddess of
Immeasurable Compassion, white in color. This yidam represents

mirrorlike wisdom and is trampling on the Demon of Delusion of Ignorance, or Demon of Birth.

► To the south is Sangwé Yungdrung, or Secret Swastika, who is the color of the sky and in union with Tangnyom Tsémé, Goddess of Immeasurable Equanimity, blue in color. This yidam represents the wisdom of equanimity and is trampling on the Demon of Death.

Mind and Prana in Meditation Practice: 12
Tsa Lung and the Nine Pranas

The rider—the mind of innate awareness—
Is mounted on the horse of mindfulness.
Propelled by the wings of the unimpeded wind,
It moves through the path of the bodhichitta central channel
And arrives at the secret door of bliss at the crown.

—FROM *THE TWENTY-ONE NAILS*, DZOGCHEN TEACHINGS
FROM THE *ZHANG ZHUNG NYEN GYÜ*

WHEN YOUR mind maintains awareness in meditation practice, it can travel a clear, direct path to higher meditative experiences. When your mind lacks awareness, it is inevitably propelled into places it doesn't necessarily want to be. It gets caught up in endless internal chatter, fixates on problems and worries, and gets dragged into anger, guilt, pride, or desire. Whichever destination your mind arrives at there is just one essential force that propels it there: the vital wind known as prana, chi, or (in Tibetan) lung. Prana is the essential energy underlying all of existence. All of the ways you can relate to the world and to your own mind, energy, and physical body are affected by prana and all are inseparable from prana.

Prana has everything to do with your ability to think and see clearly, laugh, cry, pray, digest your food, drive a car, and even stay alive. Importantly, prana is also fundamental to meditation practice. Your practice will have no effect unless your mind can touch the central issue, whether that issue is cultivating joy, purifying karmic traces, generating devotion to the master, or connecting with the most subtle experience of the nature of mind. How mind touches the issue is through prana.

How Mind and Prana Interact

To enter the doorway of the mind, therefore, you must harness and guide prana rather than be driven by it. Consciously guiding prana begins with a basic understanding of the *energy body*. Unlike the physical body, which is made up of flesh, blood, bones, cells, blood vessels, and vital organs, the energy body is made up of mind and energy: a system of spheres of light, sacred winds, channels of light, and chakras.[21] Tantric practitioners develop their awareness of the energy body in order to attain the body of the deity. Developing this awareness requires skillful visualization in meditation practice.

The Bön *Mother Tantra* uses the analogy of the horse, rider, and path to explain the relationship between mind, prana, channels, and chakras:

- ▶ **Prana is like a blind horse.** Without your mind holding the reins, prana gallops unaware in whatever direction karma forces it to go.
- ▶ **The mind is like a lame rider.** Without prana to propel it, your mind is unable to access and connect with higher experiences of freedom, openness, and clarity. It also can't effectively reach others through prayer.
- ▶ **When the lame rider catches the blind horse,** your mind can go where it intends, experience the right kind of space, connect with the right qualities, and manifest in the right ways. How does your mind catch and guide the prana? Through awareness.
- ▶ **The channels are the path.** Just as a horse will naturally follow a clear trail through a forest, prana travels through a system of channels running throughout the body. There are gross physical channels such as your body's nerves and blood vessels, subtle energy channels, and very subtle channels that are more related to mind.

---

21. For more information about the energy body and its components, see Tenzin Wangyal Rinpoche, *Healing with Form, Energy and Light: The Five Elements in Tibetan Shamanism, Tantra, and Dzogchen* (Ithaca, N.Y.: Snow Lion Publications, 2002).

▸ **The chakras are the intersections,** the energetic junctions where many channels meet.

CLEARING THE PATHWAYS

When the pathways and intersections are clear, horse and rider travel unhindered. The free flow of mind and prana can manifest in your meditation practice as a beautiful experience of contemplation, with enlivened senses and a clear and open flow of awareness. When the flow of energy in the pathway is obstructed, the higher experiences of meditation practice and the right vibration of sound syllables are not there, and your body itself may suffer from disturbing emotions and mental or physical illness.

The flow of mind and prana defines the quality of experience; in the end it comes down to awareness. When your awareness flows smoothly in the right direction, that's good. When your awareness is cloudy or blocked or it goes in unintended or unwanted directions, that is not good.

What blocks or hinders the healthy flow of prana? For one, there are *energy disturbances*, including the disturbing emotions of anger, greed, ignorance, jealousy, and pride. Energy disturbances also comprise distinctive energetic experiences that can't be tied to a given emotion—such as the disquiet you can feel for hours after awakening from a nightmare.

There are also *mental images*, which are more mind related than energy related. Look closely within yourself: Do you experience your self-image as being like a clear, open sky or is it cloudy or dusty? What slides are regularly projected in your mind?

Negative emotions can be experienced both as energy disturbances and mental images— for example, an image of your father or mother, or of the location where you experienced a traumatic event years ago. Physical illness may be associated with an image of teeming microbes or of an organ deformed by surgery or disease. Karmic forces may be reflected in the image of your "famous person" or of an ominous dark cloud.

Prana holds these images in your body. People talk of spontaneously remembering images and experiencing emotions when they receive a massage. This is because as the channels begin to open, some of the mental images and energetic disturbances are released with the prana. They are more free to come and go and dissolve into space.

Physical massage has temporary benefits, whereas working with your body, energy, and mind through regular meditation practice has more lasting, far-reaching effects. Meditation practice includes sitting with a good posture—the position of your body affects the openness of the channels, the openness of the channels affects the flow of prana, and the flow of prana affects your mind. In your practice, when the conditions are right, you can bring awareness to the images and energy disturbances, release them with the prana, and then replace the obscurations with the positive support of purer, more enlightened qualities.

Prana is as close as your own breath. Simple focused awareness on the breathing process, as practiced in insight meditation, can take you very close to your deeper self. You ride your own breath, and it takes you home. In the Tibetan Bön Buddhist tradition, there is a more sophisticated breathing practice that works specifically with the prana, channels, chakras, energy disturbances, and mental images. Called the tsa lung practice (*tsa*: channel; *lung*: prana), it opens the channels and chakras and permits the free, healthy flow of prana. A full description of this practice is given in chapter 14.

The tsa lung exercises can help you to feel more clear, grounded, open, flexible, and blissful. For meditation practitioners, the bottom line is that they improve the quality of abiding in the nature of mind. I recommend that you practice the tsa lung exercises right before doing your other meditation practices.

THE NINE PRANAS

There is not just one form of prana; actually, there are countless forms. For every type of mind or mental activity, there is a corresponding type of prana that is inseparable from that experience. The chapter of the *Mother Tantra* entitled "The Unceasing Sphere of Light" (*minub tiglé*) describes nine categories of prana that encompass the full range of experience—everything from the subtlest reality of the nature of the mind to the grossest physical forces capable of destroying the universe.

The more knowledge you have about prana, the deeper and more targeted your work with it can be, and the more far-reaching the effects in your meditation practice and your life. The nine pranas are:

1. **Prana of the space of bön nature.** This is the essence that pervades everywhere, through both matter and mind. As an abstract concept, it is difficult to grasp. You may have heard it said, "God is everywhere"; this prana is the air quality of the essence that is everywhere. It is not moving or active, it is prana in its subtlest form. One might even say that it is the potential for prana rather than a manifest state. The prana of the space of bön nature is the air quality of the innate awareness that is always present within you.

2. **Prana of the bliss of primordial wisdom.** This is the subtle, blissful air that generates wisdom. The moment you feel a deep experience of wisdom during contemplative meditation, prana of the bliss of primordial wisdom is activated. Contemplative breathing, powa, tummo, kundalini yoga, and other practices related to wisdom and inner fire rely on this prana to produce wisdom and bliss. To better understand prana of the bliss of primordial wisdom, think of a yogi who continually abides in the nature of mind with experiences of effortless great bliss. Or there may be people in your life who always seem naturally very happy and joyful, even in difficult life situations—in a sense, this is how prana of the bliss of primordial wisdom can manifest.

3. **Prana of self-arising innate awareness.** This prana causes self-awareness—the innate awareness that is aware of itself—to spontaneously and effortlessly arise. Like the first and second pranas, this one is very much related to a higher meditative state of mind. The first prana has to do with existence; the second and third have to do with recognition, or awareness, of the primordial wisdom. All three can be equated to the changeless precious body described in chapter 2. To relate to the prana of self-arising innate awareness, think of a yogi characterized by "crazy wisdom"—someone who is spontaneous and childlike, who never acts according to

a plan. Or, you may know someone who always seems flexible, able to make the best of any situation and immediately adapt to challenging circumstances without being hampered by thoughts, feelings, fears, hopes, or negative karma. If someone suggests to you "Let's go to a movie tonight!" and a little voice inside you says "Yes!" even before your first thought arises, this prana may already be activated in you. But if your instant reaction is wariness, conflict, or negativity, then spontaneous prana is lacking. Spontaneity is characterized by openness to any situation.

4. **Prana of the horse of the mind.** This is the force that speeds the flow and movement of your thoughts. It has the effect of fueling the analytical mind. Think of someone you know who is continually caught up in their thoughts, to the point of causing discomfort or harm—this might be considered the characteristic personality of the prana of the horse of the mind. Meditation practices of focused concentration, such as zhiné practice, effectively tame this prana and calm the moving mind. In zhiné one focuses as intensely as possible on a visual or sound attribute while trying not to follow the past, plan the future, or change the present. By calming the mind in this way and taming the prana of the horse of the mind, one is able to experience and become familiar with the thought-free state, the subtler aspect of mind and the deepest aspect of the self.

5. **Prana of the force of karma.** This prana propels us through transitions of life and death. It is particularly active in dream and sleep and in the bardo. While we normally have some ability to guide the prana of the horse of the mind, when the karmic wind blows, we feel we have no choice. Our thoughts migrate through the force of this prana, and the body follows. If the karmic wind is blowing in an easterly direction, we feel like moving toward the east. When the karmic wind blows up or down, it can increase or decrease the prosperity of individuals or even nations. This wind can carry the image of your "famous person"—the one who can cause you to feel, think, and act in ways over which you have little control. It's often not easy to recognize when prana of the force of karma

is at work, but a lama may see it in someone and recommend a karmic purification practice.

6. **Prana of the coarse mental afflictions.** This is the wind that carries the rough emotions, such as anger, greed, jealousy, or pride. Everyone can relate to this prana and to its effects of provoking emotional instability. When you work with releasing negative energies and emotions and cultivating positive antidotes, you are working with this prana. Purification practices such as the Six-Lokas Practice (described in the next chapter) are used to purify both prana of the coarse mental afflictions and prana of the force of karma.

7. **Prana that disturbs the humors of the body.** This is the prana that, through its excess or depletion, directly causes imbalances and diseases of the body. To improve our health, we try to release, guide, or transform this prana. For example, we work with it when we physically transform into a goddess in the elements practices in order to relieve pain or heal sickness. People who are characterized by too much humor-disturbing prana may be weak and vulnerable to illness and constantly complain of various maladies—even the idea of the flu may make them come down with it.

8. **Prana of the power of existence.** This prana is related to actions of natural law. It is what keeps the earth together, keeps the rules of the seasons, and maintains the relationship between people and the environment and the earth itself.

9. **Era-destroying prana.** This prana is capable of bringing on natural disasters. It is the cause of earthquakes, devastating floods, tsunamis, massive forest fires, and other extraordinary forces of nature that destroy the environment in which we live. Both era-destroying prana and the prana of the power of existence can be caused by collective karma, the karma that accrues as a result of the actions of a group.

Keep in mind, all prana can be thought of as fuel. As shown above, one form of prana fuels the thoughts, another the emotions, another disease, and so on. When you get rid of the fuel, then whatever has been driving you away from yourself comes to a stop. Or in the case of the first three pranas above, adding more fuel can bring you to higher experiences of mind.

TABLE 12.1 THE NINE PRANAS

Prana	Tibetan Name	Description	Subdivisions
1. Prana of the space of bön nature	*Bönnyi gyi yinglung*	The air quality of innate awareness	The Five Buddha Families: Künnang Khyapa Chétak Ngomé Selwa Rangjung Gélha Garchuk Gawa Döndrup
2. Prana of the bliss of primordial wisdom	*Yeshé gyi délung*	The subtle, blissful wind that generates wisdom	The Five Wisdoms: Emptiness Mirrorlike Equanimity Discriminating All-accomplishing
3. Prana of self-arising innate awareness	*Rigpé ranglung*	The prana that causes self-aware-ness to spontane-ously arise	Object Meaning Action Delusion Without delusion
4. Prana of the horse of the mind	*Yi gyi talung*	The force that speeds the flow and movement of thoughts	Pranas that cause the organs of the five senses: eye, ear, nose, tongue, body
5. Prana of the force of karma	*Lé gyi shuglung*	The force that propels us through transitions of life and death	Good Bad Neutral Joy or bliss Suffering

6. Prana of the coarse mental afflictions	*Nyönmongpé tsublung*	The wind that carries the poisonous emotions	Anger Greed Ignorance Jealousy Pride
7. Prana that disturbs the humors of the body	*Dubé truglung*	The prana that through its excess or deficiency causes physical imbalance and disease	Wind Bile Phlegm Combination
8. Prana of the power of existence	*Sipé toblung*	The prana that affects the actions of natural law	Pure Impure Beings Environment Bardo
9. Era-destroying prana	*Kelpé jiglung*	The wind that is capable of bringing on natural disasters that destroy the environment in which we live	Compassionate period Small collective cycles Lifespan Karma Time

THE NINE PRANAS IN PRACTICE

The teachings on prana have been put into practice by yogis for thousands of years. The nine pranas make sense to some people but remain a secret to others. For those of us who have the capacity to understand, the more we study and reflect, the more it becomes clear and obvious that prana is fundamental to meditation practice, particularly in the tantra and dzogchen traditions.

These nine pranas encompass everything: from essence of mind, to thoughts and emotions, to the grossest experiences of the physical and external environment. All nine are dynamically related. When disturbances of one kind of prana are not purified and released, the prana at other levels may be affected. For example, if you have a deficiency or an excess of the first three pranas, which are related to higher meditative states, the second set of three pranas will become more active and imbalanced. These pranas (the second set) are more energy related. If they are out of balance, then the last three pranas, which are more gross, physical, and external, may become active and imbalanced.

The entire progression from subtle to gross can even be witnessed in a single meditation practice as the effects of meditation dissolve. The higher state of benefit from meditation is like experiencing the essence (first prana). When you discover this experience of the nature, or rigpa, feelings of bliss may arise (second prana). If you abide until the bliss experience disappears, self-awareness is there (third prana). As you continue to rest in self-awareness and the effects of practice dissipate, moving thoughts inevitably arise (fourth prana). If you are unable to control thoughts and they become strong, the karmic wind may take advantage of this vulnerability and remind you of your famous person (fifth prana). As a result, emotion will arise (sixth prana). Taking the process to its conclusion, if you abandon your practice completely and become emotionally or psychologically troubled, you may become ill (seventh prana), and sickness in turn can lead to feelings of catastrophic destructiveness (eighth and ninth pranas).

It's not that it's inherently bad to have thoughts and emotions or to be sick or vulnerable; this is all part of normal life experience. But sometimes when we have too much of anything, it brings an imbalance in our health and well-being. Many patients in a cancer center are there because of the long-term effects of too much emotional or psychological disturbance. Earthquakes and other environmental afflictions can be seen as a manifestation of too much negative collective karma. Anger, pride, or other disturbing emotions can be brought on by karmic forces or an overactive mind.

Luckily, ongoing meditation practice can halt and reverse this process. If you have been strongly affected by your father's anger, for example, then when you clear the prana of the coarse mental afflictions in meditation practice, there is less room in you for the anger and more space for love to manifest. As a result there is less room for depression, sickness, or destructiveness. Clearing the disturbing emotions makes it easier to address the karmic forces underlying them and to clear the prana of the horse of the mind. When you calm the movements of your thoughts, whether through the tsa lung practice or calm abiding (zhiné) meditation, you can have more recognition of the prana of self-arising innate awareness.

If you repeatedly access the subtlest levels of awareness through the doorway of the grosser pranas, the benefits extend past this current lifetime. Nearly all of us will face strong physical, emotional, karmic, and conceptual obstacles during the last days of our lives as we start to lose every aspect of the inner and outer world we identify with. Practicing now with physical illness—whether it's a headache, a head cold, or heart disease—will help you to become familiar with releasing the disturbances and naturally abiding in awareness. Then, no matter how sick you become later, you won't necessarily lose your connection with the essence, and you will have a better opportunity for liberation.

In chapter 11, I discussed the process of connecting with the subtle space and light of the yidam Sangchö Gyelpo by entering through one of the qualities of the four immeasurables of love, joy, equanimity, or compassion. If joy or equanimity is a gateway to the center of the mandala, consider that even sickness itself can be a doorway to entering your center to become a whole person. A terminal illness can help one to remember and relate to the teachings and can completely change one's values. Similarly, as you bring sickness or emotions fully into your awareness and skillfully work with the prana associated with them, over time you can exhaust your attachment to that prana. When you fully release the prana, you discover your center.

People who are driven to achieve wholeness, whether through meditation, spiritual search, or psychotherapy, realize that the forces driving them go beyond their health, other immediate needs, or their conceptual understanding. Their focus is on a purer intention: through practice to achieve their center.

A Change of View: *Transforming Ego-Based Identity through the Six-Lokas Practice* 13

WHETHER WE are conscious of it or not, we all want to achieve wholeness. We all want happiness. We all want a deeper connection with the people around us, our loved ones, our environment, and the universe. We all are seeking to improve the worlds in which we live.

When we are looking for a positive change in our life, consider this: we can transform our entire universe by transforming our identity. As we continue the discussion of mind as a doorway to enlightenment, I would like to approach the concept of identity from the perspective of mind. This issue of identity is an important one. We have already learned that we can develop the identity of the changeless precious body. We can become the body of light. We can become the yidam Sangchö Gyelpo, the embodiment of inseparable space and light.

If you ask yourself right now "Who am I?," what is the answer? Are you a loving parent? A wise psychologist? An angry son? A jealous lover? A proud businessperson? Or are you identifying more as an open, compassionate being of light? When your identity is based more on ultimate truth, you see joy and light reflected in the people and places around you; but when your sense of self is based on dualism and relative truth, your world has more experiences of suffering and darkness. Identity based on the authentic self has the view of openness and infinite potential; ego-based identity is continually subject to boundaries and restrictions.

Not recognizing the true nature of mind is the essential ignorance from which the other two root poisons, attachment and aversion, arise.

From these three root poisons come all the other disturbing emotions. The disturbing emotions are what create the ego-based identity, and the ego-based identity in turn gives rise to all your problems in life. Your identity, therefore, is yet another doorway to enlightenment. By shifting your sense of who you are, you have the ability to transform everything for the better: your feelings, your relationships, all your experiences, even the entire world you live in.

CHANGE CAN HAPPEN

The teachings on the Six-Lokas Practice give insight into how we can take on the more authentic identity we are seeking. The Six-Lokas Practice is from the *Zhang Zhung Nyen Gyü*, a principal cycle of Bön dzogchen teachings, and is traditionally done as part of the entry into the higher dzogchen practices. I myself did a forty-nine-day retreat on this particular cycle of teachings with my teacher Lungkar Gélong when I was around fifteen years old.

Essentially, the practice involves visualizing yourself as a divine being of light called Shenlha Ökar. As this new identity, you have the ability to clear your negative emotions and transform them into enlightened qualities such as love or wisdom. It is customary in tantra to visualize self-transforming into a deity who actualizes your desired result. Just a single meditation session can give you a powerful taste of a new, higher identity; when done regularly over time, the practice also brings long-term change in your sense of self and your view of the world.

When people are feeling unhappy, depressed, or not good enough, they often feel they can't change, that they are stuck, but this is not true. Every situation is changeable, and it can change very quickly: if all the right causes and conditions meet, it is a question of days, weeks, or months, not years.

In order to self-transform into a higher dimension, it is essential to recognize that at any given moment your sense of identity is not your innate nature. Like every other life experience, your identity is subject to constant change. In fact, it is your very nature to change your identity. Think back to all the stages you already have been through in life; from infancy to young childhood, to adolescence, young adulthood, or middle age, you can see clearly that your view of the world and the way you see and think of yourself has changed many times over. Are you the same person now that you were at age five? Definitely not.

Recognizing this possibility for change is what makes people feel better when they read inspiring books or attend the teachings. But the truth is, the moment they are trapped in emotions, they believe that's who they are. And that is the problem.

One moment you might feel great, as if you are the best and most beautiful person in the world; the next moment you might feel you're in the hell realm. Or you can feel trapped in a single realm of emotions for years at a time. For example, many cities have a bad section of town, a "hell neighborhood" whose inhabitants are defined by anger. Every rusty bar on a window or piece of broken glass on the pavement conveys a sense of anger, and for the people living there, anger penetrates their sense of self. They themselves are reflections of the hell realm: they are broken, damaged, hurt, neglected, dangerous. Meanwhile, just a few miles away there may be a "god neighborhood," where every home borders the golf course and has a Jacuzzi and a swimming pool, and every resident feels pampered, balanced, and secure. The citizens of an entire nation can identify mainly with the dimension of pride, while those of another nation may experience perpetually unsatisfied hunger or greed.

The Six Realms

You can see evidence of different emotional identities everywhere you go and in everyone you meet. The Bön Buddhist tradition explains that there are six realms (Skt. *lokas*) that make up all of samsara. According to the teachings, each of the six realms is inhabited by a specific type of sentient being, and each is characterized by a specific negative emotion. We humans are said to play out our lives strictly in the human realm, where jealousy pervades our sense of identity. Clearly, however, at one time or another, each of us will identify to some degree with each of the six realms and their corresponding emotions.

The six realms are as follows:

The *hell realm* is dominated by anger. Anger manifests as conflict, tension, shouting, and violence. At its most extreme, it can lead to death or war. Anger often only serves to perpetuate our problems because it causes pain and destruction and makes us lose control and self-awareness. Its antidote is pure, unconditional love.

The *hungry ghost realm* is characterized by grasping and greed. Greed can be defined as a sense of excessive need that can never be satisfied—like trying to quench one's thirst with salty water. Greed itself perpetuates feelings of loss. Think of an addicted gambler who constantly loses, is constantly dissatisfied with any winnings, and keeps playing on and on, thinking "maybe next time . . . maybe next time." Greed is closely associated with an imbalanced relationship to possessions and sexuality, for example. People consumed by greed look outward for fulfillment but can never find true satisfaction because the loss they feel is actually lack of self-knowledge. The antidote to greed is open generosity.

The *animal realm* is dominated by ignorance. Ignorance brings a sense of being lost, of having a great need without knowing what one really wants. The ultimate sense of ignorance is lack of knowledge of self—or lack of innate awareness, *ma rigpa*—and its antidote is wisdom. But we can also think of ignorance in terms of doubt. Doubt produces confusion, distrust, fear, insecurity, and instability. The deepest doubt is self-doubt, and the antidote is self-awareness. The real sense of doubtlessness is abiding in the nature of mind, in the realization that everything is perfect as it is and that you have been complete from the very beginning.

The *human realm* is characterized by jealousy. Jealousy is the feeling of discomfort that arises when you watchfully or carefully guard something to which you are attached. The object of your attachment may be an idea, relationship, or possession. When you feel jealous, you see the source of happiness as something outside yourself. You may think, "That car (person, idea, accolades) should be mine, not yours!" Because of the closed, overly protective nature of your attachment, the antidote to jealousy is the great opening of the heart that arises from connecting to your own true nature.

The *demigod realm* is filled with pride. Pride is related to feelings of accomplishment and uniqueness. It has a very territorial aspect and seems to be particularly connected to ego and identity. Usually pride is about feeling superior, but sometimes it is about feeling inferior, like a "reverse pride." In either case we feel special and different and may feel intolerant of differences in others. The pride of the demigod realm is probably the cause of every war created on earth. Its antidote is the great peace and humility that arise from resting in one's own true nature.

The *god realm* is characterized by a lazy balance of all the negative emotions of the other five realms. This balance brings a feeling of self-centered, lethargic pleasure. A little bit of anger, a little bit of jealousy, a little bit of pride . . . all of the emotions, but just a little bit. This false harmony makes us feel that all our desires and needs are fulfilled, but something always comes along to tilt the balance. As soon as harmony turns to discord, we feel each of the afflictions stronger than ever, just as any of the other beings do. The antidote to this selfish joy is the all-encompassing compassion for all sentient beings that arises from self-awareness.

This is not to say that any of these emotions is entirely negative. As samsaric beings who are always subject to conditions and relative truth, emotions can serve us well. Even anger can energize or inspire us, strengthen or protect us—as long as we know how to work with it. We need to know the best way to be with our emotions, express them, and playfully work with them toward our well-being and enlightenment without being driven by them.

From the point of view of samsara, the god realm is the perfect place to be. Who doesn't want balance, security, and the fulfillment of all one's needs? But from the point of view of the teachings, the god realm is just another realm of suffering, and we need to go beyond it if we are to achieve true self-awareness. If you stay too long in the god realm, chances are you are not even going to the demigod realm next but will be heading right to hell. The sense of lazy pleasure gives a false sense of security and liberation; once in the god realm, it seems like everything is perfect and will last forever, but time moves quickly, and shortly before the shift happens, your whole world starts to collapse.

As you fall, you fall far and fast. There is also immediate suffering as you realize that all your beliefs about being self-illuminated and secure were based only on illusion.

Most psychotherapists may not agree with the Buddhist perspective that says it is possible to be free of negative emotions. Still, the person who has no anger, greed, or pride is truly not missing anything. Someone who is close to enlightenment simply doesn't have the same degree of emotion that exists in other human beings. If you're in that place, it's wonderful.

The dharma explains that in each of the six realms there is some cause or condition that keeps the sentient beings there from experiencing awareness of their true nature. Each negative emotion has its own action and results. Each obscures the truth. Each shuts us down to people around us and to the beauty of the moment. Each, inevitably, brings suffering.

A JOURNEY TO A NEW IDENTITY

When we recognize which realm we are identifying with, we naturally want to minimize our pain and suffering. We usually try to fix things outside ourselves. For example, when we feel like a hell being, we lash out at the person who makes us angry. Or we try changing our clothing, hairstyle, job, partner, or the town or country we live in, or even our name.

Making these external changes may help temporarily, but it will not fundamentally change our experience. For example, the hell realm will follow us to the next relationship, the next job, or the next town. In every new town we will find all the same annoying neighbors and coworkers but with new names and faces. The problem with a window in our old house will be a problem with the door in our new house. Even someone who escapes from the army to join a Tibetan monastery may find in the monastery the same boss giving orders, the same strict discipline, and the same disciplinarian he tried to escape from. The reason you experience a certain realm in your external surroundings is because the emotion of that realm is also in you. You can see only what you are—and what you are is what you see.

You may know conceptually that a problem is nothing more than a projection of your mind, impermanent, and an illusion. But as long as the emotion remains with you, it seems so real. It pervades your consciousness. When you're having a conversation, the emotion is still there. When you're watching a movie, it's still there. When you're asleep and dreaming, it's still there. As much as anything, it is there.

Our ego-based identity is very proficient at keeping these experiences alive in us. Self-image determines how we feel emotionally and energetically, how we relate to other people, and how we perceive the outer world. Only when we are truly able to change our self-image will we be able to change our view, our perception of reality. If we have the right view, there is no reason to get angry. If we have no cause for anger or destruction, when we walk through the hell neighborhood, we will not experience the threat of anger. Ultimately, with the right identity and the right view, none of the six realms will manifest.

I know I can change my identity, and I want to change because my current state does not allow me to achieve my full potential. How can I change my view and my identity? It is a matter of journeying internally into the psychological dimension, to the fields of energy where the actual identity as a hell or other being is created.

For example, imagine you are going through a very difficult time because you are very angry at someone. When you look inward, you see someone who is experiencing a hell realm. What you see is not the innate Buddha, not a being from the god realm, not a hungry ghost. It is a self who, specifically, is facing hell. Experientially, you cannot point exactly to where this self is located. When you go deep, however, you can feel the pain. You can feel it in certain locations in your body. Maybe this experience as a hell being is manifesting as physical illness. Maybe it manifests as energy. Maybe it manifests as a form of confusion or mental suffering. Even if you are feeling quite open and relaxed and are not actively angry, you still may find you are subtly connecting to this self-image as a hell being.

Just recognizing your self-image in this way is powerful because it is an opportunity for transformation. But if you can journey even deeper to find the very seed of your identity, through the Six-Lokas Practice you can clear the seed so the emotion can't grow back.

THE BEING OF LIGHT

At this time you could simply close your eyes and say, "I want to purify my hell realm." There is the "I" who is in hell and wants to purify, and there is "my hell realm" that the "I" wants to purify. But it is very difficult or impossible for a hell being to purify hell. The "I" who wants to purify the hell realm needs to be a much higher self-image, one that itself is very pure. Imagine that instead of anger your identity is one of pure love. You feel love deep in your body, in your energy, and in your mind. Imagine that you embody generosity, great wisdom, openness, peacefulness, and compassion with the same intensity. You will need these antidote qualities in order to purify and transform the six disturbing emotions and their manifestations in your life.

In the Bön tradition, Shenlha Ökar is the wisdom being who actualizes all these perfect qualities (see figure 13.1). Our practice, therefore, is to imagine becoming this divine being of light, so we can embody these qualities in ourselves. Through the power of our mind and the blessings and empowerment of the deity, we feel an immediate and profound transformation in our mind, our energy, and all the cells of our body. How well we can purify our disturbing emotions depends on how much we are able to embody the deity's qualities in a place deep within us where we feel stronger and more solid, grounded, and ripened. At the moment of transformation, we want to feel the change as clearly, directly, and strongly as possible: "Now I am the divine being of light." It is not "I think I have transformed" or "I have tried to transform"—having thoughts like these is a sign of not having the qualities of the being of light.

Normally when you bring your mind toward a certain individual—your "famous person"—the emotion of anger rises immediately and effortlessly. However, as the divine being of light, the moment you look inward and see the image of this person, your experience is different. You now have no cause for anger; instead you feel beautiful. You feel immediate compassion for the person's suffering, which comes only from their ignorance, their lack of self-realization. As the being of light and inspired by compassion, you now send rays of light out from your

Figure 13.1 Shenlha Ökar, the divine being of light (see also plate 10)

Shenlha Ökar (Shen Deity of White Light) is also known as Lhachig (Great God) in the Bön tradition of Tibet. He appears at the center of the Bön Refuge Tree (*Tsogshing*). Shenlha Ökar has one face and two arms. His hands are placed in his lap in the gesture of meditation. He is luminous white in color and adorned with the beautiful ornaments of a peaceful deity. Seated on a snow lion throne, he abides in a pure land. Shenlha Ökar manifests for the benefit of beings as the Six Subduing Shen (Buddhas of the Six Realms of Samsara) in order to guide the beings of the six realms (Tib. *kham*, Skt. *lokas*) from suffering to liberation.

heart that enter the energetic dimension of your hell realm, purify all the negative images and their environment, and perfect them.

You can go even deeper and purify the very karmic seeds of anger. There are six seeds from which arise each of the six negative emotions, and there are six seeds that give birth to the six antidotes to the negative emotions. Each seed of emotion is made up of subtle prana that is related to karmic traces. In meditation practice we use Tibetan characters to identify these karmic seeds. For example, *DU* is the seed syllable of the hell realms; when we burn our mental image of *DU*, it helps burn away our karmic image of hell.

REAL RESULTS

Once we have burned away the seed, we are a divine being who can now perfect the hell beings and the hell realms, transforming them into buddhas of love and pure lands of love. Where there used to be feelings and images of anger and hate, there are now only images of love.

After practice, real change can happen. Maybe when you actually meet your "famous person" again, you will discover you feel a little bit more openness toward him or her . . . and after a few more practice sessions, maybe also a little bit of love. These changes keep happening as you yourself begin to change.

The practice really works when one trusts in it and applies it. When I am having a real problem with somebody, doing the Six-Lokas Practice regularly over time can help me to view that person absolutely differently. I often recommend to therapists who receive these teachings that they self-transform into the being of light before seeing their patients. All these qualities of love, compassion, and openness can be valuable in their work.

You can feel a transformation in a single visualization, but without regular practice, it is difficult to achieve any kind of long-term change. For example, a woman I know had been having some major conflicts with her mother. She told me she had been wishing for her mother to be less critical and angry and more peaceful, loving, and kind. One day, she said, she had gone to visit her with the intention of improving the relationship. She traveled there filled with compassion, love, and good intentions. But as soon as she arrived at the house, the mother greeted her with a criticism: "What have you done to your hair?" Right then all her love and compassion flew out the window. It wasn't until after she had reacted as usual in hurt and anger that she remembered her reason for being there. "Yes, my hair is not that great, let's go inside and have a cup of tea," she said. But it's very exhausting for someone to try and be kind when that's not who they are.

I can imagine that if the daughter had been regularly doing the Six-Lokas Practice, her experience could have been quite different. Suppose she spends half an hour each day practicing. In each session she transforms herself into the divine being of light and evokes the image of her mother as an angry hell being; she experiences the mother's suffering; she cultivates great compassion; she burns the image and its karmic seeds; and she perfects and empowers her mother and all the other beings of the realm. At that point, the old image is gone. Her mother is vividly transformed into a loving, beautiful person. By the time the daughter goes to see her mother, she is now able to meet her from a place of spaciousness and even to find humor in the negative comments. She and her mother can have a lot of fun joking about her hair and go in and have a nice cup of tea together. It is all a bit less effortful.

Doing the practice does exactly that. It's like spending a weekend with a happy person—when you return home, the window or door that bothered you before is not so terrible after all, and the effects can support positive changes in your view for days afterward. You see your problems in a new way. Transforming into the being of light, taking on this new identity, causes these changes.

One can think of this practice as a way to overcome psychological and emotional obstacles, but one can also see a deeper meaning in it. Not only does being dominated by my hell quality prevent me from living, working, and interacting with people fully, it also makes it impossible for me to fully experience my essence, the nature of mind, the subtlest aspects of my wisdom. The deepest experience of transforming into the divine being of light is of *being* the divine being of light. This is the experience that is beyond hate and love, pride and peacefulness, and desire and generosity. It is the pervasive, boundless view that is so important to dzogchen practice.

Practices of the Mind 14

THIS CHAPTER OFFERS a variety of guided practices related to the door of the mind, although there is never a clear demarcation between body, speech, and mind. For example, the Six-Lokas Practice is included here as a practice of mind because it emphasizes the notion of identity; however, just because it's called a mind practice doesn't mean you can't do it when you need help for physical illness. In the same way, one can use every practice of the body and speech chapters, including every physical yoga posture and every mantra, as a doorway to enlightened mind. It's all a matter of emphasis.

The practices that follow begin with detailed instructions for the practice of tsa lung with the nine pranas. They continue with the Three-Sacred-Syllables Practice ("breathing light"), a simple but profound practice that helps one to achieve a balanced experience of the openness, awareness, and union that are so fundamental to dzogchen. The chapter concludes with a simplified version of the Six-Lokas Practice.

THE PRACTICE OF TSA LUNG WITH THE NINE PRANAS

The tsa lung practice, from the Bön *Mother Tantra* (*Ma Gyü*), is an excellent aid to other practices of the mind. Through a combined focus of mind, breath, and physical movement, the physical tsa lung exercises open the chakras and channels while clearing or exhausting the obscuring prana. Doing these exercises at the start of any practice session can help you to abide more easily in the undistracted, open awareness of contemplative meditation. Tsa lung also allows you to engage more deeply and powerfully in prayers and invocations.

In my teachings on the Three Doors as well as in my book *Awakening the Sacred Body*, I have consistently emphasized the tsa lung practice as a practice of the body due to its clearly physical nature. Here, we can consider it as a support practice for connecting with mind and prana as described in chapter 12. For beginners, the preliminary instructions below may seem a bit complicated, but the practice is actually quite simple. In summary, the practitioner:

- breathes in the pure air of awareness
- holds the breath in a specific chakra location
- physically exercises the area in and around the chakra
- exhales the prana through specific channels, and with it all the negative images and energy disturbances dissolve into space, and the more enlightened qualities are permitted to flow in their natural, positive directions

For the best results, read through and understand the information below. Then, just relax, do the practice, and trust that the intended experiences will arise. The more you practice the tsa lung, the easier it will be.

The five tsa lung movements are discussed in detail in *Awakening the Sacred Body*. I have described below just one of the movements. What is new here and not found in the *Sacred Body* book are the instructions for incorporating the nine pranas as discussed in chapter 12.

If you have already been doing the tsa lung movements, it is easy to adapt them to incorporate the nine pranas. The possible effects are infinite, and they can improve both your relation to the practice and the depth of your practice.

Four stages of the breath. The *life-force* tsa lung movement described below works specifically with the heart chakra—the most important chakra of the body, located in the middle of the central channel. As with all tsa lung exercises, there are four stages to the breath:

1. *Inhaling.* As you inhale, experience that the breath is actually carrying the awareness. The inhalation has a welcoming quality: You inhale the positive and nurturing aspects of air, particularly the

qualities you lack. Inhale this pure prana through the side channels and feel the central channel, particularly the heart chakra, fill
with positive energy.[22]

2. *Holding.* While holding the breath at the heart chakra, feel you
are holding all the positive qualities as a vessel holds nectar.

3. *Re-inhaling.* Re-inhalation creates the heat and energy necessary
to distribute or spread the nectar throughout the body with the
main concentration at the heart chakra.

4. *Exhaling.* At the end of the movement, exhalation exhausts,
expels, and clears the prana or winds that cause harm. As the
heart chakra and the channels are opened and cleared, the life-
force prana and other positive pranas are more activated.

The effect of movement. In each tsa lung exercise, one performs some
physical movement while holding the breath in order to generate sacred
heat and bliss. This inner heat and bliss act to "digest" the emotions
and other, more subtle obscurations so they can be more easily released
with the out-breath. Where there is no heat and bliss, the obscurations
remain stuck.

If it is difficult to hold the breath throughout the entire movement,
you can do a short re-inhalation. If that does not suffice, you can
reduce the number of repetitions of the movement. Over time, try to
build up your stamina so you can complete all repetitions while holding the breath.

The heart chakra. The heart is the palace of the divine and the abiding place of the primordial Buddha Samantabhadra. Drawing attention to and opening the heart chakra is a way for us to get closer to
Samantabhadra.

The life-force prana. The life-force tsa lung practice helps us to connect
with, activate, and permit open flow of the life-force prana, a precious
wind that is essential for achieving enlightenment. When the life-force
prana is strong, the heart chakra is open, and the person has vivid

22. A description of the three channels appears in the guided practice below.

experiences of clarity and vitality. When it is weak, the person is frail and has a clouded mind and weakened memory. If this prana is absent, death will result. When imbalanced, the life-force prana manifests as hatred and anger; when balanced, it manifests positively as happiness, joy, strong will, and the development of wisdom. This prana is white or clear in color and is related to the space element.

Choosing from the nine pranas. Besides releasing the life-force prana, the tsa lung practice also serves to release, clear, or exhaust one or more of the nine pranas as described in table 12.1. To choose which prana to work with, emphasize the one prana that most negatively affects you. Try stepping back from yourself and seeing yourself more objectively, as a therapist might see his or her patient or as a lama might see his or her student. When you do so, it may become very obvious which form of prana is fueling your experience. If you are overly critical in your conceptual thoughts, for example, you can work with the prana of the horse of the mind. If you are emotionally unstable, you can work with the prana of the coarse mental afflictions.

You may want to practice with all forms of prana over time to become familiar with all of them. In each case try to connect with the prana as clearly and vividly as possible. For example, you can evoke the prana of the force of karma by calling up a mental image of your "famous person" or another scenario that is sure to push your buttons. To connect with the prana that disturbs the humors of the body, you can call up an image of a diseased body part. See the section "Instructions for Visualizing with the Nine Pranas" below for specific visualizations for each kind of prana.

I recommend working with just one prana until you are familiar with it. Later you can incorporate a second, subtler prana into one cycle of breathing and eventually a third. I suggest three pranas in one cycle of breathing as a manageable number to work toward.

When practicing with multiple pranas, the point is to work with them in order from gross to subtle. For example, if your main issue is ridding yourself of cancer, in a single out-breath you can visualize that the disease itself is released with the humor-disturbing prana; then the emotions related to the disease can be released with the prana of the coarse mental afflictions; then the karma that caused the sickness is released with the prana of the force of karma. With each exhaustion of pranic energy, you feel a deeper and deeper sense of resting in the release. At the end, abide in the absence of those obstacles or blockages. Try to maintain awareness of that space without elaborating or changing the experience.[23]

Working with multiple pranas. When practicing with three pranas at a time, I recommend choosing the pranas as follows:

Primary problem	Pranas to focus on
Sickness or pain	7, 6, 5
Emotional crisis	6, 5, 4
Strong karmic influences	5, 4, 3
Bothersome thoughts (nonemotional, for example, excessive worrying or other fixed thought patterns)	4, 3, 2
Subtle obscurations of dullness or restlessness while meditating	3, 2, 1

1. Prana of the space of bön nature
2. Prana of the bliss of primordial wisdom
3. Prana of self-arising innate awareness
4. Prana of the horse of the mind
5. Prana of the force of karma
6. Prana of the coarse mental afflictions
7. Prana that disturbs the humors of the body
8. Prana of the power of existence
9. Era-destroying prana

Once you become very familiar with every form of prana, it is possible to work with all nine together in a single cycle of breathing (from gross to subtle). That way, just one exhalation becomes a microcosm of what happens during a long meditation session. First you are able

---

23. Such a practice should always be done in conjunction with any appropriate medical treatment.

to feel comfortable in your physical environment, then in your emotions and thoughts, and finally you are able to rest deeply in your self.

Getting the most from practice. Don't just inhale and exhale—the practice is much richer than that. Use your inhalation of pure prana to connect with a very deep place in yourself. While doing the physical movement, know that it is physically moving all of the different areas to which you have brought awareness. As you deeply exhale, feel a clearing from the grossest, most physical levels to the deepest, most subtle levels. Then, rest in the release of the obstacles, blocks, and obscurations. Feel that the practice is opening the heart chakra on many different levels.

You can feel a physical effect from the practice, then an energetic or emotional release; in the end, just be. Connecting with the space of open awareness is more important than the experiences arising in that space. Allow everything, regardless of whether it seems good or bad. You are not even trying to maintain the bliss. Bliss only comes when you are not putting in any effort.

The higher effects of the practice will come in time. Some people say that the first time they do the tsa lung practice, they connect with pain. In any kind of healing, the important first step is to encounter the disturbance that needs to be healed. At the moment of encountering there will be reactions. As the healing process continues, the effects will be subtler and subtler.

Observe the changes in yourself over time. When you remove the prana that disturbs the humors of the body, does it help you to remove the prana of the coarse mental afflictions? Does removing the emotional prana help to remove the prana of the force of karma, and does that in turn help to remove the prana of the horse of the mind?

The more you do the tsa lung practice, the subtler your results will be. Eventually, the practice will bring you to a blissful experience.

The Practice

- ▸ *Assume the five-point meditation posture.*
- ▸ *Visualize the three root channels* (see figure 14.1). The central blue channel rises straight through the center of the body and widens slightly

from the heart to its opening at the crown of the head. The side or secondary channels, one red and one white, have diameters the size of pencils and join the central channel at its base. The juncture of the channels is four finger-widths below the navel. The secondary channels rise straight up through the body on either side of the central channel before curving around under the skull, passing down behind the eyes, and opening one at each nostril. The right channel is white, representing

Figure 14.1 The three root channels (see also plate 12)

method, and the left channel is red, representing wisdom. The channels are made of light.[24]

▶ *Relax the body and inhale the pure prana* through the nostrils and the side channels. When it reaches the junction of the channels feel the positive, nurturing qualities enter the central channel. As you inhale, experience that the breath is actually carrying the awareness. Imagine this pure prana penetrates through all the blocks you feel, through your energetic experience, through your emotional pains. As you continue breathing in, imagine that this awareness penetrates through all the disturbances of the main prana you wish to clear or exhaust. Deeper than that, feel that it reaches a very deep place in your heart and in your central channel.

Hold the air within the area of the heart chakra. Re-inhale, continuously holding and maintaining the focus at the heart chakra while feeling the prana spread through your chest and nurture the area of your heart. Maintain awareness of the obstacles of the prana you are seeking to exhaust and clear.

Now perform the movement (see figure 14.2): Rotate your right arm over your head five times counterclockwise with a motion like a lasso. Feel that you are gathering vital air, which expands your chest and strengthens your life force. Then rotate the left arm over your head five times clockwise with the same lasso motion. Still maintaining the breath and the focus, place your hands on the sides of your hips and rotate the upper torso five times toward the right and then five times toward the left to generate the sacred heat and bliss.

At the end, exhale the breath out the side channels through the nose, releasing the negative prana, while the subtle prana is expelled through the heart. Feel that the obstacles are released and exhausted. With the deep exhalation, rest a moment. Feel a continuous opening of the space within your heart, and the healing radiation outward of the life-force prana. Repeat three, five, or seven times.

---

24. In previous texts, the colors of the side channels are described as being reversed for women (red on the right, white on the left), but I have found that most women relate just as easily as men to the colors as described here.

Figure 14.2 The life-force tsa lung exercise (see also plates 13 and 14)

At the end of the last repetition, remain longer in contemplation and experience the changes at the level of the body, energy, and mind. Try to maintain the absence of the obstacles, blocks, or obscurations. Rest deeply in open awareness as long as the experience remains fresh.

BREATHING LIGHT:
THE THREE-SACRED-SYLLABLES PRACTICE

The practice of the three sacred syllables helps us to cultivate the same qualities of emptiness, clarity, and union as the fivefold practice of Dawa Gyeltsen explained in chapter 10. For this reason, it is a good idea to review that chapter before reading further here.

This practice is from "The Red [or Essential] Instruction on the Three-Sacred-Syllables Practice (*népa hum düpa om dröpa a kyi martri*) of the *Oral Transmission of Zhang Zhung*. The three syllables referred to are the warrior syllables *A*, *OM*, and *HUNG*. Here, *A* represents the dharmakaya (emptiness or openness), *OM* the sambhogakaya (clarity

▶ Instructions for Visualizing with the Nine Pranas

In the breathing exercises of the tsa lung practice, different types of prana require different visualizations. *When working with more than one prana in a single cycle of the breath*, follow the breathing-in instructions for the prana of your primary focus. When breathing out, for each prana released, visualize as follows, in turn from gross to subtle:

1. Prana of the space of bön nature
2. Prana of the bliss of primordial wisdom
3. Prana of self-arising innate awareness
   For each of the above pranas:
   ▷ *Breathe in* pure awareness.
   ▷ *While breathing out*, feel that the higher meditative experiences of the prana are more present and activated within the now-open chakra and are radiating freely.
4. Prana of the horse of the mind
   ▷ *Breathe in* pure awareness.
   ▷ *While breathing out*, feel the release of the flow and movement of thoughts, and connect with the state free of thoughts.
5. Prana of the force of karma
   ▷ *Breathe in* pure awareness.
   ▷ *While breathing out*, visualize and feel that the seeds of your pride, anger, or other emotion are released and dissolve or liberate into pure space. You can visualize the appropriate Tibetan seed syllables if you are familiar with them,[1] or the seeds may be more indistinct and trace-like as a form of luminous energy. The compelling, driving force of karma is naturally released along with the seeds. If the seed of an emotion no longer exists, the emotion cannot grow back.
6. Prana of the coarse mental afflictions
   ▷ *Breathe in* pure awareness with a quality of the antidote you

1. These syllables are listed in table 14.2 accompanying the section "A Simplified Version of the Six-Lokas Practice" later in this chapter.

need. For example, if you experience anger, breathe in the antidote of love. The antidote for desire or greed is generosity; for ignorance, wisdom; for jealousy, openness; for pride, peacefulness; and for the lethargic pleasure associated with a balance of all the emotions, compassion. Besides these six emotions and six antidotes, there are other antidotes you can work with. For example, for sadness or depression, you can breathe in joy; for fear or anxiety, openness and spaciousness, or hope and trust. Be skillful in identifying the emotions that most affect you and the positive qualities that can serve as antidotes.

 ▷ *While breathing out*, release the images that are associated with the emotion.

7. Prana that disturbs the humors of the body
 ▷ *Breathe in* the essence of the five elements of nature—the positive healing qualities of earth, water, fire, air, and space.
 ▷ *While breathing out*, release whatever mental images you have related to the illness (such as an image of x-rays or of what the disease looks like within you).

8. Prana of the power of existence
 ▷ *Breathe in* the essence of the five elements of nature—the positive healing qualities of earth, water, fire, air, and space.
 ▷ *While breathing out*, release any mental images you have of disharmony between humans, the earth, and the environment, such as the effects of war, pollution, overdevelopment, or deforestation.

9. Era-destroying prana
 ▷ *Breathe in* the essence of the five elements of nature—the positive healing qualities of earth, water, fire, air, and space.
 ▷ *While breathing out*, release any mental images you have of natural disasters, such as earthquakes, floods, tsunamis, asteroid impacts, volcanic eruptions, or wildfires. ◄

TABLE 14.1 THE THREE-SYLLABLES PRACTICE

Syllable	Color	Kaya	Qualities	
A ༨	White	Dharmakaya	Openness	Emptiness
OM ཨོཾ	Red	Sambhogakaya	Awareness	Clarity
HUNG ཧཱུྃ	Blue	Nirmanakaya	Union of openness and awareness	Union of emptiness and clarity

or awareness), and *HUNG* the nirmanakaya (union). Other aspects traditionally associated with the three kayas can also be brought into the practice; see table 14.1.

Engaging the mind with the flow of breath together with the syllables is a powerful aspect of the Three-Syllables Practice. With each cycle of breath you connect with the three kayas in one single sphere. You breathe out openness with white *A*, breathe in awareness with red *OM*, and while holding the breath, abide in the union of openness and awareness with blue *HUNG*. The result is ultimately achieved when all three distinct qualities are experienced as a single taste.

Keep in mind that in dzogchen, *A* is not really white in color but has more of a reflecting quality. It is because of the luminosity of space that all the other colors can be seen. White is the simplest way to describe it.

If you don't have a good relationship with seed syllables, it is fine to practice with light instead: breathe in red light, hold with blue light, exhale with white light. Realize, however, that the practice is more powerful when visualizing the syllables. Remember the image of the mind as rider, guiding the horse of prana through the path of the channels—when you visualize a sacred seed syllable it is like armor has been provided for the rider. The syllable protects your mind from any other mental images that might negatively impact the practice and thus supports you in maintaining a higher state of mind. When you understand

Qualities (continued)			
Space	Essence	Unchanging body	Mother
Quality	Nature	Unceasing speech	Son
Manifestation	Energy	Undeluded mind	Energy

the meaning of each syllable, have the right relation to it and incorporate it in your visualization, your practice will be more powerful.

The Practice

▶ Assume the five-point meditation posture and relax your body.

▶ Become aware of the three channels of clear, luminous light within your body (see figure 14.1). A central channel whose diameter is approximately that of your index finger rises straight up through the center of the body, beginning just below the navel and widening slightly from the heart to its opening at the crown of the head. There are two additional channels, one on each side of the central channel. These join with the central channel at its base below the navel, rise straight up, curve under the skull, and pass down behind the eyes before opening at the nostrils. The central channel is blue, the channel to your right is white, and the channel to your left is red.

▶ Visualize and feel these three channels within you.

▶ Take a deep breath and exhale, releasing the stale breath. Repeat two more times.

▶ Bringing mind together with the breath, practice breathing lightly in and out through the nostrils and side channels until the flow of breath feels evenly balanced between the two channels.

▶ Draw attention to your heart at the center of the central channel. See and feel at the heart a luminous blue *HUNG*. This syllable represents the nirmanakaya, or the union of emptiness and clarity.

▸ Inhale very gently through both side channels and hold the breath. The pressure of holding causes air to enter the central channel at the junction and the blue *HUNG* to rise through the central channel. See and feel it jump up slightly above the crown of the head and begin to descend again. As you hold and connect with *HUNG* and its movement, abide in the inseparable union of emptiness and clarity. *Be* the sense of union, with a sense of comfortable, joyful, resting presence.

▷ As the *HUNG* returns to approximately heart level, begin to exhale through the nostrils. With the out-breath, the syllable descends to the base of the central channel, where it transforms into two luminous white *A* syllables that continue smoothly up through the side channels and out through the nostrils into space. These syllables represent the dharmakaya, or emptiness. As you exhale, feel and see the luminous white light of *A* filling the channels, exiting, and then spreading out into the entire universe, where it transforms all it touches into empty luminosity. The experience of *A* is relaxed, comforting, open, and luminous. It is connected to the base.

▸ As you begin your next inhalation, the white *As* spontaneously transform into two luminous red *OM* syllables, one at each nostril. These syllables represent the sambhogakaya, or clarity. While breathing in, invite the red *OMs* down through the side channels to the junction with the central channel, where the two syllables transform into a single luminous blue *HUNG*.

▸ Again, hold the breath. See and feel *HUNG* rising up through the central channel as before. Feel it rise through your heart and up above your crown and then descend. Abide in the experience of union: the union of emptiness and clarity.

Repeat from the symbol ▷ above. Send out *A*, invite *OM*, abide in *HUNG*. Repeat this breathing cycle continuously. As you begin the practice, the experiences of breathing in, abiding, and breathing out will be distinctive. Eventually, they will become more similar. The more similar they become, the better the practice becomes. *A, OM,* and

HUNG clearly have different qualities, but through the practice the three qualities should eventually become one.

For example, as the emptiness of *A* transforms into the clarity of *OM*, try to feel that the sense of emptiness still remains—clarity, after all, is only the awareness of emptiness. As the clarity of *OM* transforms into the union of *HUNG*, try to feel both emptiness and clarity in inseparable union. And as the union of *HUNG* transforms into the emptiness of *A*, try to continually maintain that sense of union within the experience of vast emptiness. Eventually, the true experience of union comes when all qualities are totally in balance, when breathing out and breathing in are almost the same. That is the real state of abiding in clear light as union.

You can do this beautiful practice anywhere: while waiting in line at the post office, sitting in traffic, shopping at the supermarket, or seated in meditation. You can't say you don't have time to breathe! In the beginning stages of practice, you take longer, deeper breaths; when you become more accustomed to it, you can breathe a little more quickly. Every time you exhale, it helps you to connect with the base and with your self. Every time you breathe in, it brings you life and awareness. Every time you hold, it brings you to an open, uplifting place of union. Done skillfully, in time you are brought to the blissful experience of one taste.

A SIMPLIFIED VERSION OF THE SIX-LOKAS PRACTICE

This section presents an abbreviated version of the traditional Six-Lokas Practice from the *Zhang Zhung Nyen Gyü* (see chapter 13). The only reason I've explained it differently from the original text is to make it simpler. It is good to begin in a simple way—simple and powerful, so one will have some experiences. Once one has a strong base in practice, one can elaborate on the practice by following the original text more closely. As with other practices in this book, this practice is best done with direct guidance from a qualified master.

A particular focus here is the self-transformation into Shenlha Ökar, the peaceful white deity who is the embodiment of love, generosity, wisdom, openness, peacefulness, and compassion. When visualizing the transformation, you should really try to allow the change to happen. Every possible opening you can make, any small door you can keep open, helps you go deeply into that experience of a new self, a new identity. Once you enter that deep place something magical can happen.

With the support of a pure self-image as the divine being of light, you will now be able to enter one of the realms, and as this being you can purify and transform the realm and its beings. How do you enter the realms? The entrance to each of the six realms is within one of the corresponding six chakras of the energy body. These chakras have physical locations: the soles of the feet, the area of the sexual organs, the navel, heart, throat, and crown of the head (see table 14.2). The physical location of a chakra and the particular form of prana that abides there support us to have the experiences of a particular realm. Consider the chakra as being like a mystical door to another dimension. Although the entrance itself has a specific location, the place you arrive at is not located physically within you. Once you enter the chakra, you find yourself in the actual realm.

For example, as an enlightened being, you will enter the hell realms through the soles of the feet with the strong intention of helping. As the divine being of light, you can see and feel all the sufferings of hell and purify the beings there. Through your blessings, awareness, strength, and clarity, all the hell beings are transformed into buddhas of love and all the hell realms into realms of love. Even the deepest karmic seeds are totally purified and transformed.

As you enter the realm, you may see many images there. You are meeting with all the people and places you associate with anger—all your hell friends, hell relatives, hell partners. You may see not only images from the past and present but also images of the future. When you see anyone in your life suffering as if they really were in a hell, you cannot help but immediately feel empathy and compassion with a sincere desire that these beings no longer suffer. Active compassion in an external hell neighborhood would be expressed through external actions, for example, you might volunteer in a soup kitchen to feed the hungry. Active compassion manifested internally would involve giving some sense of love to yourself—feeding yourself love. When angry you are essentially hating yourself; when you transform anger into love, you are supporting yourself.

The Six-Lokas Practice can be done not only for your own benefit but also on behalf of beings who are going through the bardo, the intermediate state between death and rebirth. For this reason it is traditionally done for a period of days or weeks right after a person's death.

The guided practice here focuses on anger and the hell realms. To adapt the practice for other realms, just substitute the new realm and its associated emotion, chakra, antidote, and so on (see table 14.2). For example, when practicing with pride and the demigod realm, you will be entering the realm through the throat chakra. You will see all the images of people and places that you associate with pride, feel compassion for their suffering, and purify the realm. All the demigods are then transformed into buddhas of peace, and the realm itself transforms into a land of peacefulness.

When working with several realms during one meditation session, it is best to begin with lower realms and gradually move up in this order: hell realms, hungry ghost realm, animal realm, human realm, demigod realm, god realm.

The Practice

► Assume the five-point meditation posture. Release any anxiety or tension with the breath. Relax and find your center.

► Cultivate a feeling of compassion in your heart, for yourself and for all suffering beings.

► As clearly as possible, visualize an empty throne in the space above and in front of you. This is the throne of Shenlha Ökar, the divine being of light.

► Sound the mantra to invite the deity to the throne:

A OM HUNG
A A KAR SA LE OD A YANG OM DU

A peaceful deity instantly appears on the throne in front of you. He is white in color, clad in beautiful ornaments, and surrounded by many other peaceful deities. He embodies and radiates all the pure, perfected qualities of love, generosity, wisdom, openness, peacefulness, and compassion. See and feel the presence of this enlightened being as powerfully as possible. Try to feel great joy that this being is here before you and generate devotion to him.

▶ Pray to him: "Please help me to transform into the enlightened dimension and please help all the world to transform into an enlightened society." Pray specifically for yourself and for anyone else you have in mind. At this moment, sound the purification mantra of the elements:

RAM YANG MANG

As you sound *RAM*, from the heart center of the deity, the seed syllable *RAM* emanates like a powerful firestorm of wisdom and enters through your crown, purifying your body and all your environment, burning away all karmic traces. Next, *YANG* emanates like hurricane winds of wisdom from the deity's heart, entering through your crown, filling and purifying your body further, cleansing it and all your surroundings of karmic traces. Then *MANG* emanates like flood waters of wisdom from the heart of the deity, entering through your crown, filling your body and purifying it and all your surroundings completely of karmic traces. Your body becomes like a crystal-clear vase ready to receive the teachings.

▶ Sound the mantra of enlightened body, speech, and mind:

A OM HUNG

As you sound *A*, from the deity's forehead flows a stream of luminous white *A* syllables. The syllables enter your forehead, and you receive the blessings and empowerment of enlightened body. Next, with the sound of *OM*, from the deity's throat flows a stream of luminous red *OM* syllables, which enter your own throat and give you the blessings and empowerment of enlightened speech. Then, with the sound of *HUNG*, from the deity's heart flows a stream of luminous blue *HUNG* syllables. They enter your heart, and you receive the blessings and empowerment of enlightened mind.

The divine being of light dissolves into you, and now you feel like this being.

► Sing the first mantra again:

A OM HUNG
A A KAR SA LE OD A YANG OM DU

In sounding this mantra, experience that now you not only feel like the divine being of light but you are the being of light. You have transformed completely, and so have all your surroundings. You have a new identity. Feel the difference between then and now. Feel the transformation in your thoughts and perceptions, your energy, your bones, your flesh, your blood, all the cells of your body, and all your surroundings. Focus on the shift that has happened, on the new sense of experiencing yourself as a divine being of light who embodies all six enlightened qualities and particularly *love*, the antidote to the emotion of the realm.

► Maintaining that new sense of identity, gradually draw your attention to *the soles of the feet*, the chakra location that is the entrance to the hell realms. As you focus your awareness there, experience that you are journeying directly into the realms. Allow yourself to see and feel all the blocks, feelings, emotions, and images that arise in those realms, particularly those that relate to the *emotion of anger*. Allow specific experiences that you have perceived or are now going through. Allow the image of your "famous person" to arise. Go deeper to sense the presence of the very *seed of anger, the seed syllable DU*. See all this without losing your identity as the divine being of light.

► Experience all the suffering of the realms, and feel great empathy and compassion arising in your heart for all the beings there. Sound the purification mantra of the elements:

RAM YANG MANG

As you sound the syllable *RAM*, the volcano-like wisdom fires of *RAM* emanate from your heart and enter into the crowns of all the beings in the hell realms, filling and purifying their bodies and also purifying the lands of the hell realms. As you sound *YANG*, hurricane winds of wisdom emanate from your heart and further purify the beings and the realms. As you sound *MANG*, floodwaters of wisdom emanate from your heart and completely purify the beings and the realms. The hell realms dissolve into light and become a pure land, and all the beings' bodies and minds become pure, like crystal-clear vases ready to receive the teachings. Feel the transformation of the environment and the beings completely cleared of all the *seeds of anger*.

► Now, sound the totally perfecting mantra:

A A

As you sound *A* two times, countless *A* syllables manifest in space and fall like rain onto the purified beings. The beings transform into *buddhas of love*.

► Next, sound the *mantra of the hell realms:*

A DU YANG SANG SANG

With the sound of the mantra, the entire realm is transformed into the *pure land of love*, and all the beings are empowered to become actual *buddhas of love*.

▸ As the divine being of light, feel great joy in the success of this purification practice. Sing the purification mantra as many times as you like:

A KAR A ME DU TRI SU NAG PO ZHI ZHI MAL MAL
A KAR A ME DU TRI SU NAG PO ZHI ZHI MAL MAL
SO HA
A DU YANG SANG SANG

Rest in this experience.

If you wish, at this time you can repeat the practice while focusing on another realm, emotion, and antidote quality, replacing the mantra of the hell realms with the mantra of the new realm. In this case it is not necessary to repeat the transformation into the divine being of light.

▸ At the close of your session, allow your visualization of the divine being, as well as your visualization of the realms, to dissolve completely into space.

Abide in nondual space, the pervasive, boundless view that is beyond hate and love, greed and generosity, pride and peacefulness.

▸ Dedicate the merit of your practice for the enlightenment of all sentient beings.

TABLE 14.2 THE SIX LOKAS

Chakra location	Realm	Emotion	Antidote	Seed syllable of the realm	Seed syllable of the element	Mantra of the realm
Soles of feet	Hell	Anger	Love	*DU* ད	*YANG* ཝཾ	*A DU YANG SANG SANG*
Secret chakra (sexual organs)	Hungry ghost	Greed/ desire	Generosity	*TI* ཏི	*RAM* རཾ	*A TI RAM SANG SANG*
Navel	Animal	Ignorance/ doubt	Wisdom/ self-awareness	*TRI* ཏྲི	*MANG* མཾ	*A TRI MANG SANG SANG*
Heart	Human	Jealousy	Openness	*NI* ཉི	*KHANG* ཁཾ	*A NI KHANG SANG SANG*
Throat	Demigod	Pride	Peacefulness	*SU* སུ	*DRUM* དྲུཾ	*A SU DRUM SANG SANG*
Crown	God	Lethargic pleasure (balance of all the negative emotions)	Compassion	*A* ཨ	*HANG* ཧཾ	*A A HANG SANG SANG*

Source: Zhang Zhung Nyen Gyü

In Closing

I F THERE IS just one small piece of information you can remember from reading this book, I would hope it is that the doorway to more comfort, happiness, and self-realization is always with you, here, now, in your own body, speech, and mind.

All the issues, conflicts, and emotions you get caught up with from day to day, hour to hour, or minute to minute, these are only reflections of the pain body, pain speech, and pain mind. When you can learn to draw your attention to the stillness of the body, the silence of the speech, and the spaciousness of the mind—when you can be fully aware of them and rest in that experience—your identity as pain body, pain speech, and pain mind can start to dissolve, and you can enter through these doorways to a lighter, more joyful sense of being.

So whenever you feel physical discomfort, whenever you are bothered by inner or outer voices, or whenever you are troubled by fear, tension, anger, sadness, let these experiences remind you that you have a choice: you can get lost in the pain and conflict, or you can enter through the three doors. You do have a choice in any given moment: trust in that choice. Remember that choice.

My wish is that the knowledge in this book will help you to enact some positive changes in your life. It is good to read and learn, but to actually become awakened through the three doors, it is necessary to put these teachings into practice.

May these teachings benefit all sentient beings by lessening their suffering and guiding them to final realization.

Appendix 1:
How the Conditional Body Develops

As discussed in chapter 3, the time surrounding death presents an important opportunity for achieving final liberation. After we die and the clear light of death arises, should we fail to recognize this primordial light and the first movements of subtle energy as our own self-manifestation, the samsaric body will again begin to develop. According to a teaching from the *Zhang Zhung Nyen Gyü* called "The Mirror of the Luminous Mind," the developmental process leading to rebirth is as follows: With the initial lack of recognition, the vital winds known as moving and karmic prana gradually arise from the radiance of emptiness and become grosser. Because we fail to recognize the light and these movements, the seeds of the disturbing emotions arise. From those seeds arise the five lights that are the pure form of the five natural elements of earth, water, fire, air, and space.

From the seed of anger, the white light arises. We feel attached to this white light, and the seed of desire arises. From desire, the red light arises. Because we do not recognize the union of these two lights, the seed of ignorance and the blue light arise, the seed of pride and the green light arise, and the seed of jealousy and the yellow light arise.

Next, the "cutting wind" and the "shaking wind" arise. From these winds, the great sound arises, and from that sound the great light arises. Because we have not realized the sound and light as our own self-manifestation, we are afraid. As a result of our fear, all five negative emotions become grosser.

From those gross emotions the following manifest:

- ▸ the *five inner elements*—bone, breath, body heat, blood, and flesh
- ▸ the *five locations*—heart, lungs, liver, kidneys, and spleen

▸ the *five doors*—eyes, nose, tongue, ears, and lips
▸ the *five sense objects*—visible objects, odors, tastes, sounds, and tangible objects
▸ the *five branches or limbs*—both arms, both legs, and the head
▸ the *five subsidiary channels*—eyebrows, facial hair, pubic hair, hair on the head, and chest hair
▸ the *five hollow organs*—stomach, large intestine, gall bladder, bladder, and small intestine.

The text further explains how each of the five lights passes from its physical location in the body through a specific channel of the energy body and then out through the door of a specific sense organ to connect with its sense objects.

▸ The white light, located in the heart, passes through the channels connecting the eyes to visible objects. (See the discussion of the six lamps in chapter 3.)
▸ The green light, located in the lungs, passes through the channel connecting the nose to odors.
▸ The red light, located in the liver, passes through the channel connecting the tongue to tastes.
▸ The blue light, located in the kidneys, passes through the channel connecting the ears to sounds.
▸ The yellow light, located in the spleen, passes through the channel connecting the lips to tangible objects.

TABLE A1.1. DEVELOPMENT OF THE CONDITIONAL BODY

Inseparable Space and Light

Primordial movement of radiant energy (clear light) Sound Light Rays

Lack of Recognition

5 Karmic seeds	Anger	Pride	Desire	Jealousy	Ignorance
5 Lights	White	Green	Red	Blue	Yellow

Cutting wind / Shaking wind Great Sound Great Light

Fear

5 Gross emotions	Anger	Pride	Desire	Jealousy	Ignorance
5 Inner elements	Bone	Breath	Body heat	Blood	Flesh
5 Locations	Heart	Lungs	Liver	Kidneys	Spleen
5 Doors	Eyes	Nose	Tongue	Ears	Lips
5 Sense objects	Visible objects	Odors	Tastes	Sounds	Tangible objects
5 Branches / limbs	Right arm	Left arm	Left leg	Head	Right leg
5 Subsidiary channels	Eyebrows	Beard	Pubic hair	Head hair	Chest hair
5 Hollow organs	Stomach	Large intestine	Gall bladder	Bladder	Small intestine

Source: "The Mirror of the Luminous Mind," a teaching by Tapihritsa from the *Zhang Zhung Nyen Gyü*

5 Lights	White	Green	Red	Blue	Yellow
5 Elements	Space	Air	Fire	Water	Earth
5 Types of birth	Miraculous	Egg	Heat	Moisture	Womb
5 Lokas (realms)	Hell	Demigods	Hungry ghosts	Animals	Human
5 Pure divinities	Künnang Khyapa	Gélha Garchuk	Chétak Ngomé	Gawa Döndrup	Selwa Rangjung
5 Demons	Demon of illusion	Demon of the aggregates	Demon of delusions	Demon of ignorance	Demon of death
4 Action deities	Peaceful divinities		Conquering divinities	Wrathful divinities	Enriching divinities
3 Kayas	Dharmakaya		Sambhoga-kaya	Nirmana-kaya	

Appendix 2:
The Benefits of Tibetan Yoga

THE BENEFITS OF the six "magical movements" of trulkhor (see chapter 4) are described in detail in the "Quintessential Instructions of the Oral Wisdom of the Magical Movements" and its accompanying commentary. As discussed below, each of the first five root exercises helps the practitioner to connect with one of the five natural elements, clear one of the poisons, and liberate one of the five aggregates, or the five aspects that make up the physical and mental constituents of a sentient being. These effects permit a specific wisdom quality to dawn and a buddha dimension to manifest. The sixth movement has other effects specifically related to dullness and agitation of the mind.

1. *The Athlete's Hammer* opens the channel of the space element and blocks the channels of anger. It liberates the consciousness aggregate (Skt. *vijñana skandha*, Tib. *namshé*), or all the components of the primary consciousness that are engaged with their own object. One can have the vision of the pure land of dharmakaya (*bönku*, truth dimension) and connect with the pure essence of space. The practice liberates us from the four diseases (the diseases of wind, bile, phlegm, and a combination of the three) and clears the external karmic obstacles and internal conceptual obstacles. We experience ceaseless space, and the wisdom of emptiness arises (see chapter 11 for an explanation of the five wisdoms). The truth dimension dawns.
2. *The Window of Wisdom* opens the channels of the earth element and blocks the channels of ignorance. The dimension of sambhogakaya (*dzogku*, complete enjoyment dimension) arises, and the mirrorlike wisdom is perfected. This posture liberates the form aggregate (Skt.

rupa skandha, Tib. *zug*), or everything that the grasping mind tries to perceive as form. When the form aggregate is liberated, we are more integrated with nature. As a result, we are less likely to be destroyed by natural forces such as fire, earthquake, volcano, hurricane, or flood. The complete buddha dimensions dawn.

3. *Spinning the Four Wheels* permits the pure essence of the air element to arise and blocks the channels of pride. It liberates the aggregate of compositional factors (Skt. *samskara skandha*, Tib. *duché*), or all

TABLE A2.1. BENEFITS OF THE SIX ROOT TRULKHOR MOVEMENTS

Trulkhor movement	Negative emotion/ obscuration	Element	Aggregate liberated
1. The Athlete's Hammer	Anger	Space	Consciousness
2. The Window of Wisdom	Ignorance/doubt	Earth	Form
3. Spinning the Four Limbs	Pride	Air	Compositional factors
4. Loosening the Knot	Desire/ attachment	Fire	Feeling
5. Fluttering the Silk Tassel	Jealousy	Water	Perception
6. The Tigress's Leap	Dullness and agitation		

Source: A cycle of teachings by Pongyal Tsenpo in the "Quintessential Instructions of the Oral Wisdom of the Magical Movements" from the *Zhang Zhung Nyen Gyü*

that is formed or conditioned by the mind that does not fall within the classifications of the other four aggregates. Absolute wisdom, the wisdom that knows things as they are, self-liberates, and one obtains realization and nourishment through connecting with the essence of the air element. The essential buddha dimension (*ngowonyi ku*) is revealed.

4. *Loosening the Knot* opens the channels of the fire element and blocks the channels of desire and attachment. It liberates the aggregate of

Associated dimension	Wisdom	Additional benefits
Dharmakaya (truth dimension)	Wisdom of emptiness	Liberates from the four diseases Clears external and internal obstacles The truth dimension dawns
Sambhogakaya (complete buddha dimension)	Mirrorlike wisdom	The complete buddha dimensions dawn
Essential buddha dimension	Absolute wisdom, "the wisdom that knows things as they are"	Reveals the essential buddha dimension The mandala of the three buddha dimensions dawns Strengthens and expands swift walking
Nirmanakaya (manifested buddha dimension)	Discriminating wisdom	The manifested buddha dimensions are completed The manifestation mandala dawns Generates the inner heat of tummo
Fully awakened buddha dimension, or embodiment of bodhicitta	Conventional wisdom, "the wisdom that knows all phenomena other than emptiness"	Removes lethargy Completes the fully awakened buddha dimension The five mandalas dawn
		Controls and perfects the power of prana Controls lethargy Liberates the disturbing movements of mind

feelings/sensations (Skt. *vedana skandha*, Tib. *tsorwa*), or all the secondary factors of mind that experience bliss, pain, or neutral feelings in relation with their own object. The dimension of nirmanakaya (*trülku*, manifested buddha dimension) manifests, and the discriminating wisdom develops. One masters the fire element and generates heat similar to tummo, the yogic inner heat. The manifested buddha dimensions are completed.

5. *Fluttering the Silk Tassel* opens the channels of the water element and blocks the channels of jealousy. It liberates the aggregate of perception (*samjña skandha*, Tib. *dushé*), or all the secondary factors of mind that grasp their objects dualistically. It removes lethargy. The fully awakened buddha dimension (*ngönpar changchub ku*) is complete, and the five mandalas dawn. Conventional wisdom, or the wisdom that knows all phenomena other than emptiness, develops.

6. *The Tigress's Leap* brings under control and perfects the power of prana and controls and purifies dullness of mind. The prana and mind enter the central channel, and disturbing movements of the mind self-liberate in their own place.

Appendix 3:
The Five Classes of Demons

A s discussed in chapter 7, the five warrior syllables are said to have the power to conquer the five classes of demons. According to the *Oral Transmission of Zhang Zhung*, specifically, these five classes are:

1. The *demons of the emotions.* The negative emotions are considered demons because they drive us away from our self and cause us to act in ways that accumulate negative karma. Too much attachment can lead to addiction; anger can lead to violence; any negative emotion can leave us feeling conflicted, lost, or unsatisfied. The five demons of the emotions are:
   - the demon of the water of attachment
   - the demon of the burning fire of anger
   - the demon of the darkness of ignorance
   - the demon of the mountain of pride
   - the demon of the hurricane of jealousy

2. The *demons of the aggregates.* The moment we are driven by a negative emotion such as anger or jealousy, one of the five aggregates is born in us. It is our attachment to the aggregates, not the aggregates themselves, that is the demon. The five demons of the aggregates are:
   - attachment to the *consciousness aggregate*, or all components of the primary consciousness that are engaged with their own object

▶ attachment to the *form aggregate*, or everything the grasping mind perceives as form

▶ attachment to the *aggregate of compositional factors*, or all that is formed or conditioned by the mind that does not fall within the classifications of the other four aggregates

▶ attachment to the *aggregate of feelings/sensations*, or all the secondary factors of mind that experience bliss, pain, or neutral feelings in relation to their object

▶ attachment to the *aggregate of perception*, or all the secondary factors of mind that grasp their object dualistically

3. *The demon of death.* This demon is the karmic force that brings about one's death.

4. The *demon of illusion.* Whereas the demons of the aggregates are our attachments to internal aspects of mind, the demon of illusion is our attachment to *external* sense objects, such as our desire for tastes, physical sensations, sights, sounds, and smells.

5. The *demon of the son of the deity.* This demon is one's attachment to one's possessions.

Appendix 4:
The Science of Mind

THE INTRODUCTION to part 3, "Undeluded Mind," went into some depth regarding mind-related teachings and practices of the Bön Buddhist tradition. Another issue that I have put much thought to during my years in the West and that I feel is helpful to address in the context of this book is the dual roles of science and Buddhism in achieving a happy, healthy mind. It is wonderful to see a growing collaboration between spiritual practitioners and psychotherapists, physicists, behavioral scientists, neuroscientists, and people in other scientific and medical disciplines who are working to gain a deeper understanding of the human mind and the human condition. Just in the past few years, researchers have accumulated significant findings about the mental and physiological effects of meditation that support what many meditators already know from experience.

In particular, the tsa lung and trulkhor practices of the Bön tradition have been scientifically shown to help patients who are emotionally and physically debilitated by chronic illness and its treatment. I have had a welcome opportunity to advise Lorenzo Cohen, Ph.D., and one of my longtime students, Alejandro Chaoul-Reich, Ph.D., among others, in their research on the effects of tsa lung and trulkhor in lymphoma and breast cancer patients at the MD Anderson Cancer Center. In a seven-week pilot study of thirty-nine people with lymphoma, the patients who engaged in the program that included the five external tsa lung practices and the ngöndro trulkhor practices were able to sleep better and longer and use less sleep medication than patients in a control group.[25] In a

25. L. Cohen, et al., "Psychological Adjustment and Sleep Quality in a Randomized Trial

similar study of fifty-eight women with breast cancer, the practices were associated with a reduction in avoidance behaviors, intrusive thoughts, and cancer-related symptoms.[26] Based on these findings, the National Cancer Institute has awarded MD Anderson a large grant to continue this work in a Phase 3 study of women with breast cancer undergoing chemotherapy.

In 2008 the MD Anderson-Ligmincha team started a new randomized controlled study examining the effects of a Tibetan sound meditation program (based on my book *Tibetan Sound Healing*) for treating cognitive dysfunction in women with breast cancer after chemotherapy. Forty women participated in the study, and a preliminary analysis of the data suggests improvements in cognitive functioning, mental health, and their relationship to their spirituality.

In a study published in the November 2004 *Proceedings of the National Academy of Sciences*, meditation was shown to cause positive short-term, and perhaps long-term, changes in the way the brain works. Researchers from the University of Wisconsin asked eight Tibetan Buddhist monks who were accomplished meditation practitioners and a control group of ten student volunteers to meditate on unconditional compassion. In the monks the movement of gamma waves during meditation turned out to be unusually powerful, fast, and coordinated, and their brain activity was particularly high in the left prefrontal cortex, an area associated with happiness and positive thoughts and emotions. The monks had considerably more gamma wave activity than the student volunteers even before they began meditating, and the more years of meditation experience they had, the higher their levels of gamma waves.

Other research at the University of California San Francisco Medical Center confirms that experienced Buddhists who meditate regularly don't get shocked, flustered, surprised, or angry to the degree that other

---

of the Effects of a Tibetan Yoga Intervention in Patients with Lymphoma," *Cancer* 100 (2004): 2253–60.

26. The full set of five external tsa lung practices from the Bön *Mother Tantra* (*Ma Gyü*) are described in detail in my book *Awakening the Sacred Body*. The *ngöndro* practices of trulkhor that are part of the study are from the *Zhang Zhung Nyen Gyü*; these foundational practices make up the set of magical movements that precede the six root trulkhor movements described in chapter 4 of this volume.

people do and showed that meditation practice appears to tame the amygdala, a part of the brain that is the hub of fear memory. Additional studies show that in people newly taught to meditate, psoriasis (an incurable skin disease) tends to clear up four times faster than among nonmeditators; also, new meditators have been shown to have more antibodies after receiving flu shots. A growing body of research shows the better your meditation technique, the healthier your immune system.

The point here is that the scientific community is beginning to take a more serious approach to studying the very real effects of meditation on the brain, the emotions, and the body, and the findings are opening the minds of more and more people to the healing effects of Buddhist practice.

A Meeting of Minds

Western psychology, of course, has its own contribution to make toward achieving a happy, healthy mind. On one side, the Tibetan traditions have much to learn from psychology and psychiatry. On the other side, the mental health professions can be enriched by the depth of knowledge available in the Tibetan spiritual traditions.

Some Western students of Buddhism can clearly benefit from psychotherapy. People may have buried psychological issues that become ornamented by the color and beauty of the spiritual teachings, and in skirting over these issues, they miss the importance of recognizing and going closer to them. While Buddhism offers countless ways to work effectively with challenging personal problems, therapy goes directly to specific life issues in a way that is more familiar—using the conceptual mind to heal the conceptual mind. Therapy can often be invaluable for developing a healthy ego and functioning better in samsara. However, the Buddhist teachings go much farther in helping us to balance our egos with our circumstances and relationships and to minimize the conceptual grasping mind that is the ultimate source of our emotional problems.

I personally have a deep, long-standing interest in Western psychology. In the late 1990s Ligmincha Institute offered a series of annual

"East-West Psychology" seminars with the intention of encouraging dialogue with therapists. However, these annual retreats eventually came to an end when I gained a strong sense that many participating therapists were inclined to alter the wisdom teachings for their therapeutic purposes. The field of psychotherapy has been in a continual state of flux since the time of Freud and Jung and has evolved into a profusion of different approaches to counseling and therapy. The resulting attitude seems to be "Let's change whatever should be changed in the dharma as well."

There is no question that certain aspects of the teachings need to be adapted if they are to be of real value to modern Western students, including various sociocultural elements and the language, symbolism, and metaphors used to communicate them. The historical Buddha himself emphasized the importance of giving the right medicine for the specific disease of the patient. The patient has changed, and to some degree the disease and its characteristic patterns have changed; therefore, the style of teaching needs to be changed. However, changing the methodology has nothing to do with changing the core message of the dharma. The Buddha's teachings were intended for humans of all cultures and for all sentient beings. Thus, Buddhists and therapists need to collaborate with each other in a way that is respectful of this ancient wisdom.

A Balanced Approach to Psychotherapy

At the same time I feel there are important gaps in mainstream psychotherapy that Buddhism can help to fill. For example, the therapeutic process sometimes seems rigid in its focus on mind alone. A therapist who has a more holistic understanding of mind, spirit, energy (prana), and body can be more skillful in treatment. Some patients will make better progress when the needs of their body or physical environment are addressed; others may respond best to an emphasis on body and mind, or on body and energy.

Also, just as individuals tend to be drawn more toward their dark side, Western psychology itself tends to engage a great deal with the negative. It is true that there is much more emphasis in recent years on cognitive-behavioral therapy, with its focus on developing healthier, more rational thought patterns; yet, the perception remains that psychotherapy engages far more in purifying and exhausting the negative emotions than it does in supporting the antidotes to the poisonous emotions.

It is said that when you're cultivating a garden you need to "touch the root." Touching the root means not only digging out weeds by the root but also applying fertilizer to strengthen the roots of the good plants. There's a saying in dzogchen, "The clearer wisdom becomes, the more the negative emotions dissipate." The more you fertilize your enlightened qualities, the less weed pulling you will need to do, and the less likely it is that the weeds will grow back when you let your garden be.

The Bön Buddhist teachings say there are eighty-four thousand obscurations of the mind and eighty-four thousand doors toward the liberation of those obscurations. There are six realms of suffering and six antidotes to suffering. There are five negative emotions and five wisdoms. Traditionally, practitioners are introduced first to their suffering, conditional, samsaric state and then to the specific antidote to suffering. This approach also seems important for Western psychology to follow. A Western equivalent of the eighty-four thousand obscurations of mind might be the American Psychiatric Association's *Diagnostic and Statistical Manual of Mental Disorders*. This reference has nearly a thousand pages filled with information about how to identify mental problems, everything from disruptive behavior disorders and anxiety disorders to eating disorders and sleep disorders. Now, someone should create a companion manual of all the healthy qualities of mind: a text containing everything a professional should know about identifying and cultivating joy, love, compassion, peacefulness, equanimity, doubtlessness, and other antidotes to the disturbing emotions, energy disturbances, and mental obscurations.

If such a manual existed, I can imagine an entire form of therapy emerging whose mission is to provide positive reinforcement of the innate qualities a person needs. For every session of psychotherapy that exhausts some of a person's energy or emotions through negative talk, there could be a session devoted to nurturing the aspects of the patient that are fragile, deficient, ungrounded, or weak. The therapist could be the wise, kind, understanding friend who helps the person reflect on and make positive life changes related to their essence, their spiritual quality, their potentiality, their strength, their virtue. Basically, this is a way of sounding all five warrior seed syllables—not just *A*—to help the patient mature into a healthier, more complete being.

The more familiar we become with the positive antidotes that are essential to a healthy, happy, balanced mind and the more we can practice bringing them into our life experience, the more available those antidotes will be at the times they are most needed and the less purification practice will be needed.

Actually, psychotherapists can be instruments for a cultural shift. As more and more patients and professionals learn the positive language and symbols needed for cultivating the positive, gradually the consciousness of a nation could be transformed. Imagine watching the evening news and seeing every story of a shooting, war, or corruption balanced with an antidote that gives positive, workable solutions and other inspiring good news. The possibility for this happening is real.

The Tibetan term for Buddha is *sang gyé*. *Sang* means totally purified, and *gyé* means totally perfected. What is purified? All the causes of suffering—the negative emotions, subtle karmic traces, and subtlest levels of ignorance. What is perfected? All the enlightened qualities that already exist, with infinite potential, in the clear, luminous nature of mind. Through purifying *and* perfecting one can find balance in a higher sense of wholeness.

Index